MOVE

Practical Action for Daily Leadership

JAY R. DESKO, PH.D.

Acknowledgments

The Center Consulting Group is a Christian organization with a highly trained team that is passionate about advancing leadership and organizational health. We believe this resource on practical actions for leaders will be helpful for you and your organization. We are providing this resource as an extension of our vision of advancing organizational health.

ISBN: 978-1-7923-5019-1

Layout & design by Tiehl McRoberts

Cover art by Sarah Derstein

For more information about The Center Consulting Group, visit our website at www.centerconsulting.org or call 215-723-2325.

THE CENTER
CONSULTING GROUP

Contents

Move Introduction 9
8 Actions That Will Build Trust in an Epidemic of Distrust 11
A Leader's Pledge 15
The 4 Seasons of Leadership That Every Leader Will Experience . . 16
5 Reasons We Can (& Should) Be Optimistic Today 20
I Am Usually Right & You Are Always Wrong 23
Is Your Vision Sustainable? 30
Leadership Fraud: How to Know When Someone Is a Fake 35
Finish Well 39
A Mistake Was Made, but It Wasn't My Fault 42
5 Gifts to Leave the Person Who Will Take Your Place 47
7 Signs of the Self-Destructing Leader: Are You One? 49
6 Traits Needed in Every Member of Your Team During a Crisis . . 53
15 Things That Will Deplete Your Credibility Bank 57
6 Deadly Miscalculations & How to Avoid Them 58
4 Questions to Answer Before Choosing Your Next Job 62
5 Things Often at Work in People's Lives Behind the Curtain 63
The Common Occurrence of Blind Spots & How to Correct Them 67
10 Reminders for Leaders During a Crisis (& Other Times) 71
Leaders & Managers: Is There REALLY a Difference? 76
6 Tips to Avoid Leadership Burnout [Hint: Don't Work Less] 78
Top 5 Reasons People Are Promoted & Fired 81
Cheating Our Way to the Bottom 82
Trust: The Element of Leadership You Cannot Afford to Ignore . . . 86
7 Life Principles That Will Not Let You Down 91
How the Mighty Fall: 6 Ways We Can Self-Destruct & Not Know It 94
How to Handle Confrontation with Compassionate Candor 96
Not All That Spreads Is Bad: 6 Things That Spread Positivity 99
7 Insecurities That Can Hold Good Leaders Back 102

Critical Thinker vs. Critical Person 104
How to Vaccinate Your Org. From Dysfunction & Decline 105
15 Disciplines That Will Strengthen Your EQ 107
10 Things Deceptive Leaders Do to Fake Their Way to Success . . . 111
How to Get More Done, Empower Others & Guard Against Overload 116
The 6 Greatest Fears Leaders Face & What to Do About Them . . . 120
5 Actions That Can Make You "Exceptional" 124
Sexual Misbehavior Isn't the Only Way to Ruin Your Life 127
Questions Every Leader or Owner Should Ask During a Crisis . . . 130
Are You Emotionally Tone-Deaf? Here Are 10 Ways to Tell 133
6 Standard Approaches to Leading. 134
Top 10 Ways to Derail Momentum and Growth 137
5 Daily Actions of Leaders That Will Be Positively Remembered 142
How to Know You Are NOT a Narcissistic Leader. 144
6 Signs of Your Organization's Shadow Side & How to Contain It 146
The Influential Leader 148
5 Positive Ways Suffering Shapes Us 150
7 Leadership Labels: Which Are True of You? 152
6 Times When You Should NOT Make a Decision 154
5 Types of People You Will Encounter in Life. 156
When to Quit & When You Should Think Twice 159
5 Reasons Why Toxic Leaders Get Away With It 162
"Trust Who?" What to Do When You Lose Trust in Others 165
How to Become a Visionary Leader 169

About

Who We Are 172
Our Solutions. 173
Assessment Tools 174
About the Author 176

Index by Topic

Career Planning

4 Questions to Answer Before Choosing Your Next Job. 62

6 Tips to Avoid Leadership Burnout [Hint: Don't Work Less] 78

Top 5 Reasons People Are Promoted & Fired. 81

When to Quit & When You Should Think Twice 159

Challenges of Leadership

The 4 Seasons of Leadership That Every Leader Will Experience . . 16

Finish Well 39

The 6 Greatest Fears Leaders Face & What to Do About Them . . .120

5 Positive Ways Suffering Shapes Us 150

5 Types of People You Will Encounter in Life. 156

Culture and Trust

8 Actions That Will Build Trust in an Epidemic of Distrust. 11

I Am Usually Right & You Are Always Wrong. 23

15 Things That Will Deplete Your Credibility Bank. 57

5 Things Often at Work in People's Lives Behind the Curtain 63

Trust: The Element of Leadership You Cannot Afford to Ignore . . .86

Not All That Spreads Is Bad: 6 Things That Spread Positivity 99

5 Daily Actions of Leaders That Will Be Positively Remembered 142

6 Signs of Your Organization's Shadow Side & How to Contain It 146

"Trust Who?" What to Do When You Lose Trust in Others 165

Effective Leadership

A Leader's Pledge 15

5 Gifts to Leave the Person Who Will Take Your Place. 47

6 Traits Needed in Every Member of Your Team During a Crisis . .53

Leaders & Managers: Is There REALLY a Difference? 76

7 Life Principles That Will Not Let You Down 91
How to Handle Confrontation with Compassionate Candor......96
Critical Thinker vs. Critical Person 104
How to Get More Done, Empower Others & Guard Against Overload 116
6 Standard Approaches to Leading.............................134
The Influential Leader 148
7 Leadership Labels: Which Are True of You?.................152
6 Times When You Should NOT Make a Decision 154
How to Become a Visionary Leader.............................169

Failures of Leadership

Leadership Fraud: How to Know When Someone Is a Fake.......35
A Mistake Was Made, but It Wasn't My Fault 42
The Common Occurrence of Blind Spots & How to Correct Them 67
Cheating Our Way to the Bottom 82
How the Mighty Fall: 6 Ways We Can Self-Destruct & Not Know It 94
10 Things Deceptive Leaders Do to Fake Their Way to Success...111
Sexual Misbehavior Isn't the Only Way to Ruin Your Life........127
5 Reasons Why Toxic Leaders Get Away With It 162

Planning

Is Your Vision Sustainable? 30
6 Deadly Miscalculations & How to Avoid Them 58
10 Reminders for Leaders During a Crisis (& Other Times).......71
How to Vaccinate Your Org. From Dysfunction & Decline.......105
Questions Every Leader or Owner Should Ask During a Crisis...130
Top 10 Ways to Derail Momentum and Growth 137

Self-Management

5 Reasons We Can (& Should) Be Optimistic Today 20
7 Signs of the Self-Destructing Leader: Are You One? 49
7 Insecurities That Can Hold Good Leaders Back 102
15 Disciplines That Will Strengthen Your EQ 107
5 Actions That Can Make You "Exceptional" 124
Are You Emotionally Tone-Deaf? Here Are 10 Ways to Tell 133
How to Know You Are NOT a Narcissistic Leader 144

“

Leadership is practiced
not so much in words
as in attitude and
in actions.

HAROLD S. GENEEN

Move Introduction

Have you ever noticed how successful people have certain things in common? They take risks. They make hard decisions. They seek advice. They fix problems. They build teams. They take action. In other words, they make a MOVE! There is a reason that football has a play clock and basketball has a shot clock. Even chess has a clock! Why? Because the game cannot be won, and would become quite boring, without people making moves.

The same is true for leaders. Every person with leadership responsibilities makes multiple moves every day. They analyze, discuss, evaluate, reflect, pray, engage, decide, execute, and change. In short, they MOVE. The Apostle Peter said it this way, "Get your minds ready for action..." 1 Peter 1:13. This book is a collection of articles that were written for leaders just like you. It does not matter what you lead, where you lead, or who you lead; you are expected to take action each and every day.

There are 52 articles covering a variety of topics to help you make positive movement in your life and leadership. The book does not need to be read in sequence, although you are free to do so. But you can also read and reflect upon one each week. Or consider looking at the table of contents and reading about the topics most relevant to you at this moment. Consider using it as a discussion or training tool within your team. Regardless of what approach you take, just be sure to MOVE!

8 Actions That Will Build Trust in an Epidemic of Distrust

Who can you trust these days? According to a recent study by the Pew Research Center[1], not too many people. The survey found that Americans are struggling with trust. For example, the following percentages of Americans noted having *little or no trust* in...

- Elected officials (63%)
- Business leaders (57%)
- News media (52%)
- Religious leaders (38%)
- Police officers (31%)

Trust is tricky. Millions of people may not trust elected officials, tonight's news, or a religious leader, yet tens of thousands will trust scammers who tell them they owe money to the IRS or that there is money waiting for them in a Nigerian bank! According to the U.S. Government[2] (if you trust them), there were 1.4 million reports of fraud in 2018, and younger people fall for scams even more than older people do. So we DO NOT trust politicians, business leaders and pastors, but we DO trust a guy in Nigeria, whom we have never met, enough to send him money!

---

1 Pew Research Center survey of 10,618 adults, "Why Americans Don't Fully Trust Many Who Hold Positions of Power and Responsibility." Nov. 27-Dec. 10, 2018.

2 Witt, Paul. "The Top Frauds of 2018." Federal Trade Commission Consumer Information, Feb. 28 2019, www.consumer.ftc.gov/blog/2019/02/top-frauds-2018.

While trust can be tricky, here are eight actions that will help build trust in an epidemic of distrust.

1. Start with trust.

Have you ever heard someone say, "I will never trust them again!"? Those are the words of a person who has been hurt and disappointed. But, if we consistently start with distrust, it will result in distrust coming back to us. In other words, distrust breeds distrust, and trust breeds trust. While this may appear to be counterintuitive, even when someone has violated our trust, we must discerningly and cautiously trust once again or they will never be able to rise above it.

2. Show genuine concern.

I recently read a story of a hospital administrator who was watching how the medical staff treated her father. She felt like they spoke about him but never asked him what he wanted. They cared about his health but not so much about the rest of him. People trust those who genuinely care about them. So often, leaders live emotionally distant from those around them. This results in lower trust.

3. Spend time together.

I once had a negative view of another leader. I had perceptions of him that were, to say the least, unflattering. But due to a change of circumstance, I had the opportunity to get to know him. And we became good friends! By spending time with him, I got to know him in a better and more accurate way. That is the benefit of spending time together.

4. Do what you say.

Politicians and most others who are trying to land a job have a propensity to make promises, some of which will be impossible to fulfill. For example, politicians promise to lower taxes and provide more services. Is that really likely to happen and succeed in the long run? Leaders promise to be "team-centered" and "collaborative" but sometimes fail to do so. If we want people to trust us, we would be wise to do what we say.

5. Tell the truth.

One lie can erase years of telling the truth. This is true in all relationships including work, marriage, and friendship. As a leader, I can tell the truth three hundred times, but if I fudge it or straight-out lie once, the three hundred times of truthfulness will be forgotten, far overshadowed by the one lie.

6. Be transparent.

One of my clients and good friends is a master of being transparent. He is quick to stand in front of others, even large groups, and acknowledge his mistakes, fears, and failures. And the result is that hundreds of people love working for him and many leaders seek him out for counsel. Why does transparency build trust? Because it shows others that you trust them with your less impressive aspects and that you are human. People appreciate knowing you are like them – imperfect.

7. Be competent.

Competence is essential to forming trust, but it most often builds trust only when a certain skill set is needed. For example, when my daughter needed brain surgery as a child, we were not expecting to have the surgeon become our BFF. We just wanted the best surgeon we could find. He was definitely a world-class neurosurgeon but with a personality that was a bit intimidating and cold. I had full confidence in him as a surgeon. And that was all I was looking for.

8. Be realistic.

No one manifests being trustworthy 100% of the time. All of us eventually disappoint, forget something important, make a major mistake, etc. Perhaps one of the challenges we face in experiencing declining trust is not just people acting in untrustworthy ways. It may also be that we have unrealistic expectations. Since we are broken, none of us will succeed if the expectation is perfection. As the writer of Ecclesiastes accurately states, "Surely there is not a righteous man on earth who does good and never sins," Ecclesiastes 7:20.

A Leader's Pledge

As a leader, your actions drive the health and culture of your team. I shared the following pledge with my team, and I encourage you to share it with yours to help increase your team health. Feel free to modify it to fit your specific context.

1. I will create an environment for my team that is safe, resulting in a sense of belonging.
2. I will show gratitude for my team with both my words and deeds.
3. I will be appropriately vulnerable with my team by modeling transparency.
4. I will aspire to take less credit for success and more responsibility for mistakes.
5. I will seek genuine relational connection with my team.
6. I will pray weekly for specific members of my team and for their specific needs.
7. I will strive to speak the truth to my team – always in a spirit of love and respect.
8. I will look out for the interest of my team rather than just myself.
9. I will laugh with my team by prioritizing the importance of having fun while working hard.
10. I will monitor the cultural health of my team as much as the financials of my organization.
11. I will seek feedback from members of my team on how I and our organization can improve.
12. I will share this pledge with my team and encourage all of us to "lean in" to it together.

The 4 Seasons of Leadership That Every Leader Will Experience

My car seat is cold. Pumpkins are everywhere (my dog saw one the other day and thought it was about to attack). And Home Depot has their Christmas decorations out! The seasons are changing – summer is gone, fall is here, and winter is quickly nearing. Over the past 35 years of leading and coaching other leaders, I have observed that, similar to the seasons of weather, leaders also go through seasons. Here are the four seasons of leadership that every leader will experience.

Summer

Friends, barbeques, corn hole, and the beach. Just like the summer season in life, this is the leadership season where everything feels like it is going great. When you are in the leadership season of summer, you often feel excitement, energy, and even somewhat invincible. During summer, it is hard to even imagine that as a leader, you will one day have to contend with the cold, dark, lonely days of winter. I can recall specific seasons of my leadership life that were summer – everything was going perfect. All lights were green. Relationships were strong. And organizational growth felt limitless. That is what summer feels like! It is so exciting, and yet not even close to realistic to think it will stay that way forever.

Characteristics of leaders in the season of summer: High adrenaline, organizational growth, consistent success, and feeling invincible.

Fall

For as much as we cannot wait for summer, we always look forward to the change into fall. Brutal heat is gone. The colors are great. No more watering gardens. And goodbye lawn mower. Just like in nature, fall is a great time to prepare for the eventual return of winter in leadership. During fall, there are fewer hurricanes, snowstorms, and ice (except for California where brutal fires never seem to be out of season). In this season, leaders often feel both anticipation and enjoyment. While not as exhilarating as summer, fall is a time of anticipation for the holidays, football, and a warm fire. Leaders seldom succeed in the long run if all they experience is the adrenaline of summer or the darkness of winter. Fall is a time of steadiness and stability. I was recently talking with a leader who had over 35 years of business success in senior-level positions of large corporations. He was still very motivated, but his focus had transitioned from his professional advancement to helping others grow and advance. In other words, he was motivated and content. That is what fall often feels like.

Characteristics of leaders in the season of fall: Personal contentment, steadiness and consistency, and a sense of peace.

Winter

During winter, everything appears dead. After a few months of ice, snow, wind, and darkness, it's easy to be tricked into thinking that nothing is left. It's silent and lifeless. But it isn't. While some things go dormant, there is life below the surface of it all. The same is true for leaders. You may feel depressed, beat down, uncertain, and lack confidence and new ideas. But winter can play a vital role in the growth of leaders. It humbles us (we really do need that sometimes), and it reminds us of our limitations and dependency. I was in a meeting with a leader who had been knocked down hard over the past few years. In contrast to summer, nothing was going right, life felt dark and confidence was low. He was in winter, and it was a lonely place to be.

Characteristics of leaders in the season of winter: Doubt and uncertainty, loss of confidence, nagging sense of fear, and low motivation.

Spring

Spring is a season of renewal and growth. Just as we don't go directly from winter to summer in our natural seasons, we seldom do so in our leadership seasons. After a winter season of leadership, spring is a much needed and welcomed gift. It is during this season that a leader will begin to experience renewed hope, personal and professional growth, and the return of both vision and confidence. I recently talked with a young leader who was just coming out of a very hard time in life. After the breakup of a difficult relationship, she was looking ahead to a better season of life. She was coming out of winter and very much looking forward to the refreshing air of summer to once again return.

Characteristics of leaders in the season of spring: Personal learning, experimentation, planning and preparation, and a sense of anticipation.

Regardless of which season you are in right now, you would be wise to acknowledge it and even embrace it. You will go through many seasons of leadership many times in your life. And in contrast to our weather, you may skip seasons altogether and, for example, go right from summer to winter. There is a lot to learn about yourself and a lot to learn from others during every season. But you do not want to stay stuck in any one season for too long – seasons are not supposed to be permanent.

5 Reasons We Can (& Should) Be Optimistic Today

This past summer, my garden looked amazing. And I had little to do with it. Tomatoes. Snap peas. Tomatillos. Sweet peppers. Zucchini. Sunflowers. Jalapenos. All looking like a picture out of a Farmers' Almanac. So then why was it that my eyes often missed the greatness of my garden and instantly went to the few weeds that slipped in?! 99% of the raised beds looked fantastic, but when I walked through the garden every day, my eye instantly found those one or two little weeds! It is not that I missed the beauty or fruit in the garden. It is just a matter of where I chose to focus. Optimism is like that. We should not necessarily ignore what is broken, but we should also find what is good in the midst of it. Sometimes we focus too much on the broken over the good. So here are five reasons why we can and should be optimistic today.

1. It sure beats pessimism.

Remember Eeyore, the donkey character on Winnie the Pooh? Pooh says, "What a lovely day, isn't it?" And Eeyore responds, "If it is a good morning, which I doubt." What a way to start your day! Who has ever succeeded in life by focusing only on what is broken? Think of a chronic pessimist. Does he have people lined up who want to follow him? People who want to work for him? Who give to his cause? Who desire to hang out with him? An overabundance of pessimism is deadening not only to the carrier but also to the people whom they sometimes infect. Think of it this way – an ounce of optimism can provide fuel for another day or week or year. But an ounce of pessimism can poison a healthy culture.

2. Something good is always present.

Few people have perfect mental health, physical health, marriages, relationships, and wealth all at the same time. But all of us do have something good to see and to celebrate. Perhaps your business is in a season of struggle, but you made payroll again and you have some great people on your team. Or, maybe you are battling cancer, but you at least have the finances to cover your medical expenses. If you search for good, it is always there.

3. People can and do change.

When I turned 60, my neighbors, the fun group that they are, covered my yard with signs... 60 of them! Each with a different phrase. My favorite one said this: *"The best part of being sixty is that you did all your stupid stuff before the internet."* While I still do some stupid things, I don't do nearly as much. That sign is a great reminder that people can and sometimes do change for the good. And that is worthy of optimism.

4. Heroes still exist.

In my opinion, it often feels like TV news and most news feeds really like to focus on the dark stuff. To test my assumption, I opened one of my apps that collects news stories from multiple sources. Only one story out of four was about something encouraging or hope-generating. As I was looking, I saw the story of a man who rescued a young woman who was drowning off of the New Jersey coast. He could have found many reasons not to act, but instead he chose to be a hero. Despite the toxic news, heroes still do exist. And that is cause for optimism.

5. Grace abounds.

You may be familiar with the story about the woman who called the police on the man who was watching birds while in Central Park. She claimed he was threatening her, which was not true. After being fired from her job and being crushed on social media, she was then arrested for making a false police report. I do not know the man she accused, but I was impressed by his response; it was so gracious. He told the District Attorney that he has no interest in supporting a criminal case against her and does not hold any ill will towards her, believing she already has paid a high enough price for her mistake. God shows us extraordinary grace by withholding the penalty we deserve for our own failings. How cool is it when we see that modeled in our relationships with others? Such grace is another reminder of why we can be optimistic.

6. Your turn:__________.

What is another reason you can think of for us to be optimistic today?

I Am Usually Right & You Are Always Wrong

How is it that people, including many who are very intelligent and respectable, can see topics like work performance, circumstances, relationships, justice, and the world so differently? While it may be disturbing, it is not surprising. Although some may not like to acknowledge it, it is very common for most of us to see our world through the lens of "I am usually right, and you are almost always wrong!" Our worldviews, our brains, and the perceptions we form make us very complicated people but also predictable. Here are the primary reasons for why we see things the way we do and how we can learn to better understand other's perspectives.

How Our Perspectives Are Shaped

While many forces shape the way we see the world, here are six of the main ones.

1. Our parent(s).

I read a book written by a young woman who was raised by a family that was deeply enmeshed in an extreme fundamentalist church (extreme is an understatement). They did such horrible things that just about everyone defined them as evil. It was a fascinating story of how powerful parents are in shaping how we see the world and how hard it is to change that view. She loved her parents and trusted them. And from a very young age, these parents deeply embedded some unhealthy views of God, the Bible, and how to treat people who were different than her. When she began to see cracks in her worldview, it resulted in excessive amounts of internal stress and conflict. Change is possible, but it can be scary and difficult, especially if you may be betraying those who raised you!

2. Intense events.

Have you ever noticed how intense events stick with us and shape us more than positive events do? Over 45 years ago, I was walking our dog Fluff. (I know, not the most original name, but stay with me). I did a dumb thing and took him off of the leash while we were walking past the home of a neighbor with two German Shepherds. Needless to say, this meeting of dogs did not go well, and they came close to killing Fluff! We have had big dogs my whole married life, but to this day, I NEVER let my dogs out of my gated yard without a leash. EVER! Just ask my family – I become a drill sergeant when anyone even hints at the idea. Why? Traumatic events get deeply embedded in the brain and shape behavior for years to come.

3. Our brains.

As humans, we need to make sense of our experiences. So, when too much contrary information starts to flood in, our brains need to do something about it. Just like the stock market, the brain does not like too much ambiguity. Dr. Edward de Bono describes how our brains create patterns that, over time, are used to make sense of information, serving as a filter. A "normal" person may take his dog to a field and let him run around and it will be an enjoyable experience. But with my legacy of trauma, all the scenarios in my mind lead to a very unpleasant dog fight. In another example, a manager may fire an employee because of poor performance, but the employee cannot see it. It does not match the patterns and beliefs the employee has formed about himself. The longer we believe something, act on it, and the older we become, the harder it is for the brain to accept that there might be an even better way.

4. Our social networks.

Remember, when you were a teenager, how your parents always warned you about those whom you spent time with? They knew that peer influence is powerful, and not only for teens. Most of us are shaped by the people we spend the most time with – by how they live, what they value, who they respect, and even what they purchase. They soon occupy a space in our heads, sometimes shaping our choices and actions. Influencing one another is normal… and sometimes healthy. That is, until such influence hinders us from caring about others, hearing others, and unfairly labeling others. Do not underestimate the way you are shaped by those whom you spend the most time with.

5. Our temperament.

I am a believer that God created every person with unique traits, gifts, and thought patterns. We can be similar to others, but when you add our temperament to the other forces I note above, you can see how we are all a bit unique. Our temperament has to do with the way we think, work, and relate to others. Some love detailed work while others do not. Some love to take risks while others prefer safety. Some love working with people while others prefer working alone. Everyone likes to talk about the benefits of having diversity on a team, but in reality, we really do like it more when people think like us! So, when you wonder how people can see the world so differently, don't forget about the power of temperament.

6. Defensive Routines.

Many years ago, I knew of a person who fought hard for a particular doctrine in his church. Those who did not agree with him were labeled "liberal" and those who did were considered "orthodox." And there was no need for discussions since he was right and others were wrong! This type of labeling can be a form of defensive behavior that over-simplifies our world and justifies our actions. We all have defensive routines that kick in unconsciously, just like how our eyes automatically close when something gets too close to them. After all, people want to protect themselves from anything they perceive is a threat, but sometimes things we label threats are not. Defensive responses that are common to all of us include denial, labeling, blaming, attacking, withdrawing, and justifying. Even though defensive routines are common for everyone, they can hinder learning and growth and be an accelerant for conflict.

5 Steps to Expand Our Perspectives

These six forces that shape us do not have to be fatalistic or deterministic. As leaders, we should aim to continue to grow. Here are five actions we all can take to counter the downside of thinking only we are right.

1. Acknowledge you are broken.

I just finished reading a book about the fall of Enron called *The Smartest Guys in The Room* by Bethany McLean and Peter Elkind. The Enron scandal was one of the largest corporate bankruptcies in American history with employees and shareholders losing billions of dollars. The writers concluded with this: "The Enron story will always be relevant: It's a tale of human nature..." This aligns well with the words of Jeremiah, the Old Testament prophet, when he said, "The heart is deceitful above all things and beyond cure. Who can understand it?" None of us are completely righteous or perfectly pure in the way we think or act. For those of us from a Christian faith and worldview, we especially need to acknowledge this, be grateful for God's forgiveness, and act humbly as a result.

2. Talk with yourself before others.

For many, it is an unrealistic expectation to ask that their first step is to talk with someone with whom they may disagree. Many people are conflict avoiders by nature. Instead, start with yourself. Ask yourself, "Why do I think what I think and believe what I believe about ___________? What has contributed to my beliefs and perceptions? How did I come to hold my beliefs about this subject so strongly?" If you cannot talk to yourself about it, the odds of succeeding in talking with someone who holds a very different perspective are about the same as winning the lottery... or lower.

3. Challenge yourself.

You are not being disloyal to your beliefs if you seek to read or listen to someone who thinks differently about those beliefs. You are testing your assumptions. This is called LEARNING! But sometimes it is less threatening to do so in the privacy of your own mind. Perhaps there is a Netflix documentary, Ted Talk, article, or book you can explore. This is much harder to do than it sounds since most of us run from anything that embraces a different perspective from our own. Just recently, a good friend encouraged me to read a book that both he and I know will not align with some of my beliefs. But I did add it to my reading list since I both trust him and need to be stretched more often.

4. Resist labeling.

Labels serve a purpose. They help us to simplify life by forcing a large number of people and perspectives into a small number of labels. But that simplification process can miss the full story. Labels are very insufficient for most people. We do not appreciate it when people lump us into a category of their choosing by assigning us a label such as "dogmatic," "liberal," "lazy," "legalistic," "loser," etc. While everyone uses labels, we would do well to catch the tendency early and resist it quickly.

5. Talk with someone different.

A fascinating study was done by Dr. Paul Zak[3], a neuroscientist at Claremont Graduate University. He found that when we intentionally build relationships and show vulnerability, it releases a chemical called oxytocin in the other person's brain. And that chemical helps them to trust us! When we pursue relationships

---

3 Paul J. Zak, "The Neuroscience of Trust," *Harvard Business Review*, November 27, 2019, https://hbr.org/2017/01/the-neuroscience-of-trust.

with people who may think differently than us and show appropriate vulnerability in our conversation with them, it helps to foster trust. In addition, when we do not have a relationship with someone, it is easier to dismiss and even dehumanize them. But once we get to know them and hear their story, we start to have a greater appreciation for them, even if we don't see things the way they do. Relationships require both parties feeling safe, sharing honestly, and accepting that having different perspectives does not always mean that one person is right and the other is wrong.

It is not easy to move from "I am always right, and you are usually wrong," to "You and I can both be right and wrong," but it is possible. And it all begins with learning how we form our perspectives and how we can also change our perspectives, or at least appreciate how others may hold views that are different than our own.

Is Your Vision Sustainable?
10 Ways to Ensure Your Organization Can Withstand the Unpredictable

Bad things happen when we least expect it. The economy turns upside down. Enrollment in your school declines. Registrations in your camp go flat. A new technology results in a rapid decline in your business. Your pastor unexpectedly dies. While not everything is predictable, we as leaders should know that our organization's sustainability is only one step away from an economic downturn, a loss of a key staff member, or an unexpected change in competition or market preferences.

Think about this quote published by The Harvard Economic Society on Nov 16, 1929: "A severe depression like that of 1920-21 is outside the range of probability." Even the best and brightest can fail to see what is emerging in front of them as this was stated at the start of the Great Depression! In Proverbs 27:12, we are reminded that, "The prudent sees danger and hides himself, but the simple go on and suffer for it." In other words, wise leaders PREPARE in advance for what is coming and then ACT accordingly. Here are 10 ways to make your vision more sustainable.

1. Compelling Vision

When the unexpected happens, people get anxious, fear takes root, and a culture of darkness can begin to dominate. Sustainability requires first and foremost that you have a compelling vision <u>before</u> the unexpected happens. It is this very vision that will be vital in fueling momentum and inspiring hope. Yet, there are far too many organizations whose vision does not pass the test of being compelling in terms of tangible results. We must remember that our organizations are not guaranteed eternal life. They often rise because of a compelling vision, and they often decline when the vision is no longer compelling and unifying. As leaders, we must not focus on survival, but instead on our vision and why it is worthy of sacrifice.

2. Attainable Vision

What do you do with 82,000 acres in a desert? Not much. In the late 1950s, two very intelligent men speculated on real estate and bought this land to build what they called California City. They built roads, installed utilities, and sold a number of lots. But the project never went further than a small number of homes and a few commercial enterprises. It was not an attainable vision. There are plenty of examples of churches, nonprofits, and businesses that oversold but under-delivered on their vision. A sustainable vision is one that is not only compelling, it is attainable. Otherwise, it will never become more than a dream.

3. Awareness

As leaders, we need to be aware of what is happening around us in culture as well as in our unique field of work. Sometimes those closest to the business may also have the most clouded view of what is emerging. For example, retail stores watched but dismissed the emergence of online retailers like Amazon, and university faculty laughed at education being delivered any way other than in the classroom. Their sense of invincibility resulted in a lack of awareness – and the price was costly. External perspectives of board members or consultants can help avoid nearsightedness.

4. Cash Reserves

Crises will hit. That is certain. It is only a matter of when, not if. Those organizations that have financial reserves are not only better positioned to survive, they are also better equipped to make the most of the opportunity. As an example, organizations should have a minimum of 3-6 months operating reserves in savings. The specific amount will be influenced by the unique nature of your organization, debt-load, borrowing capacity, and revenue sources. Without such reserves, an organization will have to make sudden and often ill-advised decisions which may result in even further decline. And you can't always count on banks or donors for help during a crisis.

5. Succession Plan

People have moral crises. People have accidents. People die unexpectedly. And even if they are fortunate enough to avoid these sad events, they eventually retire and move on from the organization. Yet, it is estimated that 60% of people still do not have a will! Something that is so simple and extremely beneficial! And I would say at least that many organizations do not have a plan of what to do in the event of a sudden loss of a leader or a plan for the leader's positive retirement from the organization. Yet without both "emergency" and "anticipated" succession plans, the likelihood of long-term sustainability goes dramatically down.

6. Focused Spending

You would think that during a major crisis, the number one goal is to cut spending. WRONG. The number one goal is long-term viability for our organizational vision. While making cuts is often a necessary step, it is not the end, it is only a means. The real goal is to focus the limited resources on those activities that are most essential to our vision. And if cuts must be made, the top of the organizational chart cannot be ignored. Servant-leaders do not look out only for their own interests, but for the greater good.

7. Waste Prevention

The longer an organization exists, the more it tends to develop bloat such as wasted spending, over-staffing, and blurred focus. This, on top of not seeing the signs of change, can be deadly. Bethlehem Steel once employed 300,000 people. In 1973, they opened the extravagant Martin Tower corporate headquarters, yet only 14 years later, it was almost empty and the company was on a high speed track to bankruptcy. The longer an organization exists, the harder it is to control costs and focus energy on what is most critical to the vision. Organizations would be wise to continually assess and prevent egregious spending before a crisis, but in the event of a crisis, elimination of waste will be essential.

8. 10/20 Rule

Every nonprofit, business, and church should have a plan for reducing expenses BEFORE it is needed. Most organizations can reduce by 10% without causing excessive pain or harmful impact to the vision. Reducing by 20% takes a lot more work and a lot more courage. But it is important to create these plans. While most activities and positions provide at least some value, we need to focus on eliminating those services or positions where the value may not justify the cost. Remember, the goal is not just reducing to survive. Rather, it is freeing up some capital to invest in those aspects that are most essential to a sustainable vision. It's about good stewardship!

9. Wise Counsel

When the pressure is on, human nature tilts in one of two directions: avoiding hard decisions or making impulsive decisions that may compound the problem. A successful plan for mission sustainability can be enhanced by objective professional guidance. An experienced coach or consultant can help you test assumptions, know what questions to ask, and provide you with both encouragement and accountability to make hard decisions. Proverbs 11 says, "There is safety in counsel." Not asking for help during such challenging times is like a person having a heart attack but afraid of spending the money for an ER visit – unwise and potentially deadly.

10. Courage

Winston Churchill said, "Fear is a reaction. Courage is a decision." Show me an organization that is thriving and has a sustainable mission, and I will guarantee the leaders are making hard decisions. It takes courage to focus spending and develop succession plans. It requires courage to seek advice. And courage is always needed to make the changes necessary to adapt to shifting trends and conditions.

Leadership Fraud: How to Know When Someone Is a Fake

745,355. That's how many prescriptions a fake pharmacist was accused of approving or filling. For over 10 years, this person also gave vaccinations, supervised techs, and even advised patients about their medications, and did so as an employee of a major pharmacy chain. And she wasn't even a licensed pharmacist[4]! She is not alone in being a fraud. Many people claim to be someone they are not by faking or inflating who they are. And this includes plenty of leaders, managers, and even pastors. Here are six signs that someone is a fake.

1. Talkers

This is what I refer to as a gasbag – they talk far more than they deliver. (I could not find a better word and the other options would have been deemed offensive by some☺).
They talk a good talk and are never at a loss for words, but their leadership and track record don't seem to match those words. Fake leaders haven't yet learned, "The more talk, the less truth; the wise measure their words." Proverbs 10:19.

2. Deceivers

Fraudulent leaders often have gaps between what they say and what they actually do. I remember reading a published article by an author I knew, and I also knew what was

4 Mihir Zaveri, "A Fake Pharmacist, 745,000 Prescriptions and a $7.5 Million Settlement," *The New York Times*, Feb. 4, 2020, www.nytimes.com/2020/02/04/health/walgreens-pharmacist-lawsuit.html.

written was inaccurate. It was so inaccurate that I even called the publisher to question their judgment regarding publishing information that had never been verified. But the publisher felt it did not matter! The fraudulent leader not only deceived the reader, but the publisher also gave further credibility to the fraud.

3. Blamers

Fake leaders are notorious for shifting the blame to others when something fails. They are a bit like Teflon – nothing ever sticks to them. Declining numbers? Not their fault. Deficits? Someone else's failure. Time for a layoff? Everyone is on the line – except himself. I remember listening to a nationally known leader tell the story of how his organization ended up in trouble after a major expansion, resulting in the laying off of almost 40 employees. But he never took any responsibility for getting them into that situation in the first place. Why? He had mastered the art of blaming.

4. Exaggerators

Fake leaders are infamous for over-inflating their accomplishments. As one employee of the White House painfully learned, there is a big difference between a certificate from a university and a degree. I remember reading the online biography of a person I knew from the past. He claimed to be a major factor in the past success of an organization, but he never even mentioned the person who was the key player (and no, it wasn't me)! What he said wasn't 100% false – but it was ridiculously inflated!

5. Hiders

Fake leaders often keep others who are smarter or better at a distance. They hide behind the mediocre or average. Why? Because it is hard to hide your fraud when sharp people are around. I remember watching a leader who had become the newly appointed head of an organization. She circled herself with a combination of nice but inexperienced and mostly mediocre managers at a time when the organization needed an "A" team. Fake leaders are skilled at hiding their incompetence by shunning top talent and also not allowing people to get too close, thus keeping their mystery and illusion well nourished.

6. Deflectors

Have you ever watched a talented magician? How did they make that bird come out of the woman's ear?! They deflect your attention away from what they do not want you to see. Some fake leaders are so good at this that it is as if they are magicians themselves! They skillfully use their words and even sleight of hand to mesmerize those around them. There is nothing wrong with being inspiring. That is a true gift. But those who are genuinely inspirational focus your attention on the vision. Those who deflect direct your attention away from their incompetence and even pathology.

As leaders, we are imperfect, and we all fall short. Somewhere in our journey, we have braggingly taken the credit or weakly blamed others for a failure for which we were at least partly responsible. The difference between the imperfections of many leaders and the fake leader is the chronic nature of the person's inconsistencies and damaging behavior. Sometimes they know they are doing it, but it is often such a deeply embedded part of who they are that they no longer are aware of it. It is like their skin – they wear it 24/7 but do not pay much attention to it. It's just part of who they are.

When you see someone regularly manifesting one of these six traits (and usually more than one), you may be watching a fake leader. Fake leaders can change, but not easily. Change takes humility and a deeper understanding of what is driving their behavior. Don't write them off. If you see a window of openness and teachability, take the chance to talk with them about what you see and how you desire to help them grow into being the leader you know they can become.

Finish Well

Layoffs are accelerating. Unexpected retirements are growing. Millions of people are having to make decisions that will determine if they finish well or finish poorly.

When someone does not finish their position well, it makes it harder to successfully move on to the next chapter of life.

But finishing well is easier said than done.

Here are a few suggestions if you (or someone you know) are facing this time in life right now.

Fight the temptation of self-preservation.

It is so natural to look out only for ourselves. But those who finish well fight this tendency. Self-preservation is as natural a response as swallowing, but when it becomes a dominant motivation, it never results in finishing well.

Invest in younger leaders.

Regardless of whether you are retiring, being laid off, or being pushed out, it is our job to invest in younger leaders. People invested in us, and we owe it not only to them but also to the long-term health of our organizations to invest in others.

Never burn bridges.

Burning bridges may be a good strategy in war, but it never leads to a good outcome when we are leaving a position. It is common to feel angry or victimized when involuntarily leaving a position, but trashing your organization or its leaders will follow you and your reputation.

Investigate new opportunities for your talents.

Everyone needs a mission in life. Whether you are retiring or leaving to pursue a new opportunity, carefully consider your talents and your passion. People do better leaving when they know where they are going and what they are going to do next.

Seek advice from others.

Have you been laid off? Seek counsel from others who have experienced this and landed on their feet. Retiring? Learn from those who are a few years ahead of you on the retirement road to avoid missteps and capture all of the possibilities that can be ahead.

Help others by documenting and sharing information.

Whatever your job, you know things others do not know. You have information the organization will need. It would be easy to say, "Not my problem," especially if you feel you are being wronged, but that is taking the low road.

Work to stay engaged to the very end.

This is as hard as not burning bridges! Once you know you are leaving, it is so hard to stay focused and keep your head in the game. But those who finish a position well stay engaged. They don't coast to the finish line. They continue running to the final day.

Expand your network.

Your emotional health, job opportunities, and meaningful activities emerge from your network of relationships. While it is wise to keep your relational network vibrant, it is essential to do so during times of change. Those who finish well often do so because of the support of the friendships they have developed.

Look ahead financially.

Both retirement and forced downsizing can create a lot of anxiety and stress. And much of that comes from the questions "Do I have enough money to retire?", "Do I have enough money to take a pay cut?", or even "Do I have enough money to handle the time it will take to find a new job?" To finish well, seek out guidance from a trustworthy financial planner.

Love your people by putting them ahead of yourself.

Don't be one of those people who make a transition even more difficult by making it awkward. You know what I mean. Blessing over blame. Grace over guilt. Joy over cynicism. In other words, those who finish well focus on loving others rather than punishing them.

A Mistake Was Made, but It Wasn't My Fault

Mistakes happen… a lot. A kid is forgotten and left on a school bus. A medical doctor is dragged off of an airplane even though he has a ticket ("mistake" is a very inadequate word for this one!). A teacher uses duct tape to keep a child in a chair (really?!). A world leader has an affair with the wife of his top military leader and then has him killed to cover it up (yes – David, King of Israel). A teenager puts a smoke bomb in his neighbor's front door (I confess, this one was me). Mistakes happen and are almost always a result of human error – which means they aren't going away anytime soon. While we need to strive to prevent as many mistakes as possible, we also need to respond appropriately when they happen.

In their exceptional book, *Mistakes Were Made (But Not by Me)*, social psychologists Carol Tavris and Elliot Aronson explain that when faced with perceptions or data different from our own, we have a strong propensity to dismiss, discredit, or distort both the perceptions and those who hold to them. They note, "Most people, when directly confronted by evidence that they are wrong, do not change their point of view or course of action, but justify it even more tenaciously. Even irrefutable evidence is rarely enough to pierce the mental armor of self-justification." The following are some of the most common reactions when confronted with an error and a few suggestions for better ways to respond.

5 Common Reactions to A Mistake

1. Deny

Denial is an outright claim that it wasn't you that made the mistake. "It is not true." "I was not involved." "I don't know anything about that." These are just a few phrases that may come into play when someone is denying responsibility. When we make a mistake, denial often emerges from an unhealthy blend of fear ("I don't want to get fired") and pride ("I don't want people to think less of me"). Denial can begin to eat away at us and, when we do it often, it will harden us so we can no longer differentiate between what is true and what is not.

2. Soften

When confronted with a mistake, rather than outright deny it, we sometimes tend to soften the error by minimizing it as well as the impact it had on others. A few softening phrases are "Well, it could have been much worse," or "What's the big deal – it wasn't all that bad." Softening often disrespects those harmed by the mistake since it downplays the damage and the resulting emotions others are feeling.

3. Blame

Blaming others is often the go-to routine when a mistake is made. If denial is no longer an option, why not blame someone else? Blaming may be in play when you hear phrases such as "It wasn't me, she did it," or "I did not instruct him to do that, so I am not sure what he was thinking." Blaming is used to take the optics off of yourself and place that negative attention on someone else.

4. Ignore

Want to really infuriate someone that was on the receiving end of a mistake? Ignore them. Don't respond to her message. Ignore his emails. Refuse to meet with him. This is especially common when large bureaucratic organizations make a mistake and refuse to respond to a customer complaint. Infuriating is an understatement! When hurt people are ignored, they want to be vindicated, and they want accountability. And sometimes, they feel the only recourse is through litigation. Usually, ignoring is not a wise strategy.

5. Shift focus

If blaming shifts the attention off of yourself and onto another person, shifting focus takes the attention off of the error and onto another topic. Like an escaped criminal being tracked, this strategy is designed to throw people off of your scent! When someone is shifting focus away from a mistake, you might hear phrases like "Well, you aren't perfect either. Remember when you _____." Or perhaps, "I feel we have bigger issues to deal with than this, like _______." Some people can become very talented at smoothly shifting focus away from their mistakes and onto another topic or the mistakes of others.

2 Better Ways to Respond When a Mistake Is Our Fault

1. Own it

The Bible reminds us that we are responsible for our own conduct (Galatians 6:5). Saying "I made a mistake, and I am sorry for how it has affected you" makes a huge difference. It's that simple. If it is a serious error that involves liability, your insurance carrier will want to weigh in. And it is wise to have legal counsel. But sometimes, owning it reduces the risks since people often pursue legal remedies when they feel they haven't been respected or acknowledged.

I was listening to an interview on NPR between a director of nursing at a hospital and a woman whose baby died in the care of that hospital. A mistake was made when one of the nurses accidentally disabled an alarm which resulted in the loss of the child. Rather than blame or deny, the director of nursing and the hospital took full responsibility. Amazingly, the mother never sued, and she and the director of nursing have maintained a personal friendship to this day. Sometimes, owning an error deescalates both the situation as well as the hostility that can rapidly grow when a victim feels that we are denying, blaming, or ignoring.

2. Correct it

While it's always best practice to prevent mistakes from happening, the next best thing we can do is to make things right. In other words, fix the mistake. If the mistake resulted in missing someone's expectations, we should strive to exceed them when making corrections. Several years ago, I was co-leading a summer event for high school students where we arranged for them to serve in inner-city communities. One of the projects we had arranged ended up being poorly run and did not meet the high school group's expectations. When the leader told me about this, I was disappointed that we had not succeeded in our mission for this particular group. While I could not fix the project at the moment, I did provide the group with a significant discount when they joined us the following year (they were regular attenders). They were appreciative and satisfied. The project was ours. We were the ones who planned it, and we had to own it. We were therefore responsible to correct it to the best of our ability.

5 Gifts to Leave the Person Who Will Take Your Place

Everyone likes gifts, especially really nice ones. And that is true for your successor. As a leader, you choose what you will leave for the next person. Here are five gifts that the person who takes your place will really appreciate.

1. A healthy department or organization

Picture being told that you have just been given a house from your favorite uncle. But the thrill turns to distress when you walk through it and realize it is a disaster! You would not like to inherit a mess of an organization and neither will the next leader. You need to lead as though your child would be the next leader – working to create a healthy organizational culture that will serve as a great platform for her.

2. A great team

Every hiring decision you are making now will result in either a gift or a curse for your successor. Recruit the best and proactively prepare them for your transition. If you have people who need to move on, you need to handle it. Don't leave that painful task as the first thing the new leader will need to do. That would be a very cruel gift for him or her and a sign of your weakness.

3. Financial well-being

How would your kids like it if their inheritance was no money at all or even worse, a big pile of debt? Your successor will feel the same if you leave your organization in debt. Work to reduce or eliminate the debt and even build up a cash reserve so the new leader will have the resources to try some new initiatives.

4. Not hanging on too long

No leader feels they are hanging on to their position or organization too long, but many do. And others may not be willing to tell them so, for fear of hurting their feelings or worse – being punished. When you hang on too long, you harm the very legacy you are trying to create and you also become the theme of a lot of offline conversations – and no leader wants to be *that* person!

5. Freedom from meddling

The person who takes your place does not need you meddling in his or her new role. Regardless of what you think about him, leave him alone! Once you leave, stay away unless your opinion is requested. And even then, be cautious! You would not have appreciated someone looking over your shoulder, and neither will he.

7 Signs of the Self-Destructing Leader: Are You One?

As leaders, none of us are immune to behaviors and thoughts that can ultimately lead to self-destruction. As a consultant, I have watched many leaders, including pastors, head slowly but surely towards a crash, taking their organization along with them. And the scariest part is they do not even know it's happening. The following are seven signs of a self-destructing leader. In most cases, more than one sign is present before the crash takes place. Do you see any of these signs in your life?

1. Pride

We often hear Proverbs 16:18 quoted: "Pride comes before destruction." And guess what – it does, and research continues to prove it! From Jim Collins's book on *How the Mighty Fall* to Dr. Mortimer Feinberg's writing on *Why Smart People Do Dumb Things*, all remind us that a self-destructing leader is often standing on a foundation of pride, and this pride contributes to all of the other signs of self-destruction noted below. I recall a time when a board member wanted to hire us to help an organization plan for succession, but the top leader put the brakes on it. Why? Because he believed he knew better than everyone else!

2. Fear of feedback

One pattern of behavior I have often seen is that self-destructing leaders avoid feedback at all costs. Suggest a 360 feedback assessment, and they find 101 reasons why not to do it. They fear that what they hear may shatter the image they hold of themselves and may weaken their control of the organization. I remember one leader who, after completing a 360 feedback assessment, expressed serious anger. He could not accept that his team members were providing him with valuable critique, and he would not listen to their input. And, he eventually destructed.

3. Taking credit for success

Self-destructing leaders love to take credit for all of the success. Why? Because it reinforces the broken view they hold of themselves: they are the cause of all of the success that their organization has experienced. And, they believe if someone else is contributing to this success, it may weaken their position and control and people may start to value others more than them!

4. Blaming others for mistakes

"It is always someone else's fault." That is the motto of the self-destructing leader. They have an image to maintain and, even though it is one built on self-deception, the self-destructing leader works hard to keep it going. This is often done by blaming others for anything that goes wrong.

5. Punishing those who disagree

Like a dictator in an authoritarian regime, self-destructing leaders have a habit of punishing and banishing those who challenge them. This can include marginalizing, demonizing, or even firing. The end result is pretty much the same – people learn to not tell the king that he is naked! Many employees have told me that they don't want to share their thoughts with a leader because they have seen too many people punished for doing so!

6. Isolation

This is what some psychologists refer to as emotional distance – keeping the majority of people far enough away from your personal life and thoughts to maintain the illusion of success. After a leader has destructed, we often hear statements from clients like, "She was a private person," or "We have never been to his home." Such leaders compartmentalize their lives, separating public from private with very high firewalls. The self-destructing leader is a lot like the wizard in the Wizard of Oz, just a little flawed human hidden behind a curtain using a lot of special effects!

7. Mental health issues

According to the Substance Abuse and Mental Health Services Administration, there are over 42 million Americans[5] living with some form of mental health illness. I know many leaders who struggle with anxiety or depression and have gotten the professional help needed to manage it. However, some leaders have either an undiagnosed or unmanaged mental health issue which can result in destructive choices.

As leaders, every one of us has likely struggled with one or more of these signs. The difference is that a self-destructive leader manifests more than one sign and they have become a pattern of his or her behavior. As a consultant, I have seen self-destructive behavior showing up especially

---

5 Beth Han, Sarra L. Hedden, and Rachel Lipari, "2014 National Survey on Drug Use and Health," Substance Abuse and Mental Health Services Administration (SAMHSA), Sept. 2015, www.samhsa.gov.

in leaders who are in their mid-fifties and early sixties. Some of them have led well for many years but are now showing cracks in how they think and lead, with sad results. If you are a self-destructing leader or you either supervise one or work with one, an experienced coach can provide the guidance you need to bring about healthy change.

6 Traits Needed in Every Member of Your Team During a Crisis

Every leader is only as good as the team he or she has recruited. Certainly, that is not a new concept. But the changes that result from a crisis, like the COVID-19 pandemic, will re-define the traits needed by members of successful teams. Here are the six essential traits I believe you will need in every member of your team to successfully move forward from a crisis.

TRUST – It never goes out of style.

Many leadership theories have emerged over the years (and some have also disappeared). Great man. Theory X. Theory Y. Situational leadership. But trust will always serve as a foundation for every healthy relationship and team. When you trust your team, you do not have to be suspicious about them working remotely, or being loyal, or wisely managing resources, or taking care of constituents. Trust does not mean perfection, but it does mean being consistently dependable and credible. And it requires giving people the same benefit of the doubt you would want to be granted to you.

GRIT – Yes, it is a real thing.

What separated the leaders, students, families, and organizations who caved in from those who stepped up after the COVID-19 pandemic? Grit - the ability to persevere. It is a powerful ingredient of life that is free, available to everyone, and differentiates finishers from quitters. Some examples of grit throughout the pandemic include organizations going from physical offices to remote work in less than 24 hours, churches quickly going from face to face ministry to innovative ways of caring and connecting, and first responders running into the battle rather than away from it. Grit is a real thing, and it will matter now more than ever.

SELF-MANAGEMENT – It makes a major difference.

People are coming into jobs and teams with increasing amounts of emotional stress and personal life issues. This is true for all employers including church staff and nonprofits as well as businesses. This is not new – throughout history, people have experienced pain and carried "baggage." But we have increasingly seen that people's ability to manage this baggage appears to be declining, and it is having a real impact on their lives, careers, and on those with whom they work. Everyone, including those of us who lead, must take seriously the importance of both being aware of ourselves and our issues and learning to manage these issues. This is called self-management.

NIMBLENESS – It's not a nicety; it's essential.

I turned 60 recently. And although I regularly exercise (yes, I know some of you may find that surprising if you have ever seen a picture of me), no matter what I do, my body is pathetically inflexible. I mean like a piece of wood... or thick metal! My lack of physical nimbleness can easily lead to injuries. Likewise, if our leadership minds or the minds of our team members do not remain flexible, we will experience a different kind of injury, but just as painful.

The challenges we are facing will not be the last. The more nimble we are, the faster we can make adjustments to accommodate the unexpected.

FOCUS – It really does keep us on a better path.

No doubt, crises require attention. Things change fast. News is unending. "Solutions" are constant. Social media chatter spikes. And leaders and teams can easily become distracted. But the problem is that our primary mission can get side-tracked. The needs of clients or customers can take a distant second place. Energy and resources can get expended on things that feel urgent while other important things get neglected. Want an exceptional team? Model focus. And I know what I am about to say will cause some to cheer and some to jeer, but our country, our organizations, and each of us individually would experience a major leap forward in relational, emotional, spiritual, and political health and civility if we took a 30-day fast from social media and focused that time on reflection, mission, and on caring for others in tangible ways rather than on talking "about" and talking "at" from the safety of a keyboard. "Not gonna happen," you say? Likely not. But I know that leadership effectiveness is significantly influenced by our ability to stay focused.

MINDSET – It determines attitude.

Proverbs 27 says that we become what we think. We sure are living in a unique time (that word seems a bit weak and inadequate at this point), but I have a choice. I can focus my mind on how "everything" is broken (but it really isn't) and "everyone" is wrong (but that is an over-reach). Or I can focus my mind on what is also right or good, including relationships, clients, my team, my family, and that I have a very forgiving God. Mindset is all about us becoming what we think. Negativity generates more negativity. Cynicism generates more cynicism. But hope generates more hope. And grace generates more grace. Especially now, we need leaders and team members who practice mindset management.

15 Things That Will Deplete Your Credibility Bank

Credibility is very easy to lose but takes work to build and maintain. Why? Because credibility withdrawals for unfavorable behaviors are often greater in magnitude than the deposits for favorable behaviors. Here are 15 things that will quickly deplete your credibility bank and subsequently chip away at your leadership influence.

1. Having insufficient knowledge
2. Ignorance
3. Careless research
4. Inaccurate information
5. Outdated data
6. Lack of follow-through
7. Empty/broken promises
8. Hypocrisy
9. Duplicity
10. Pretense
11. Lack of authenticity
12. Minimization
13. Exaggeration
14. Selectivity/bias/omission
15. Dishonesty

Many of these credibility destroyers can be avoided or the behaviors can be changed. A coach can help you identify areas for improvement and create a plan for leadership growth and development!

6 Deadly Miscalculations & How to Avoid Them

"I don't think Corona is as big a threat as people make it out to be." This quote by the acting chairman of the Council of Economic Advisors, Tomas Philipson, was made on February 18, 2020. Within one short month of this statement, our country and the world were experiencing a catastrophic disruption of a magnitude few have ever experienced before. This can be summed up in one word: miscalculation. We are all fallible people, and as leaders, we have all likely made miscalculations somewhere, sometime. Here are six of the most common miscalculations and how we can avoid them.

Miscalculation #1: Your words.

If you have ever gone to a gun range for target shooting, you have an appreciation for the phrase, "Ready, fire, aim." Dumb and dangerous may be a good summary of that strategy! And the same can be true with our words. Using the wrong words at the wrong time with the wrong tone is a serious miscalculation, often with unintended consequences.

So, think first, speak second. Parents often tell their children to "use their words". In reality, sometimes we need to use fewer words if the words we are going to use are more harmful than silence.

Miscalculation #2: Your decisions.

On numerous occasions, our consultants have sat down with leaders to do an after-action review of a decision that had unintended consequences. This includes decisions such as expansion, hiring, and firing. We often tell our clients that one miscalculation in hiring can result in the loss of $250,000 or more. Trust me. We have seen this happen… a lot. Our decisions have consequences.

So, as Proverbs 15 says, *seek counsel* before you make important decisions.

Miscalculation #3: Your finances.

It did not take long from the start of the Coronavirus crisis to realize many families, businesses, and nonprofits were going to quickly come up short on cash. Various factors contribute to this – some within the control of people and some not so easily controlled. But the lesson is real regardless of the cause: a miscalculation in finances can result in little to no margin when a crisis hits.

So, it is never too late to consider where and how you can build a personal and organizational financial model that is sustainable. While cash may not be king, it is certainly essential for long-term viability and planning.

Miscalculation #4: Your planning.

Last year, a few members of our team and I were in Canada visiting an organization that is doing amazing work. Both our Associate Director and I NEVER like to be late, and we have NEVER missed a flight in all our years of consulting together. This is because we always leave plenty of time for the unexpected. Like getting a flat. Experiencing an earthquake. Or me using the restroom seven times on the way. Well, we did not leave as early as I had wanted to get back to the airport. And yes, we missed the flight due to a massive traffic jam.

So, plans should always include scenarios of things that could happen that could impact your goals.

Miscalculation #5: Your health.

When I was 30, a white cream filled donut was my breakfast of choice most mornings on my drive to the college where I was teaching. This, along with working three jobs and doing graduate studies, did not equate with looking like Dwayne "The Rock" Johnson. To be sure, I miscalculated the importance of managing my health gauge which resulted in gaining weight that I had to work extra hard to lose two decades later.

So, don't underestimate the long-term effects of the physical and spiritual lifestyle decisions you are making right now. One way or another, there is always a cumulative effect.

Miscalculation #6: Your relationships.

Have you noticed how people often fall in love quickly but how their marriages unwind slowly? Or how you build a great connection with a friend but it eventually hits a wall? How does that happen? To start, there are a lot of pressure points on relationships. Friends have different personalities, people experience geographic changes like a move, and sometimes people's values change resulting in distancing. Compounding those, marriages include additional pressure points like financial pressures, health issues, and kids. But I believe one of the greater risks to relationships is miscalculating the impact of what damage can be done when conflict is ignored, disinterest grows, and hairline cracks are not tended to.

So, don't underestimate the pressure and stressors that are common to every relationship. Keep talking. Be quick to ask for help and slow to give up.

4 Questions to Answer Before Choosing Your Next Job

Whether you are 22 or 52, there is a very good chance that you will experience a time when you are trying to figure out "what next"? Over the past 20 years, I have talked with many different men and women, both younger and older, as they wrestle with decisions regarding whether to stay at a job or leave or which out of two or three options may be best. For some, it is exciting! But for others, it can be a confusing and anxiety-producing time, especially if they make a mistake. Here are four questions that can help you as you think about both your present position as well as your possible next job. While each person may weigh these differently, our experience has demonstrated that to ignore any one of them will likely result in future dissatisfaction.

RELATIONSHIPS
Who will I be working for and with, and how much will I enjoy these relationships?

JOB
Will the nature of the job fit with my strengths, passion, and personality?

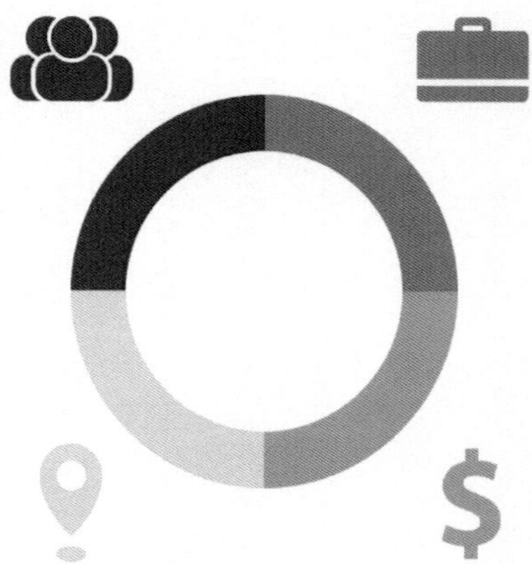

LOCATION
Will the location be a good fit relating to my needs? (medical, temperature, schools, aging parents...)

COMPENSATION
How much will I be paid, will the needs of my family be met, and will I be satisfied?

5 Things Often at Work in People's Lives Behind the Curtain

Just like the wizard in the Oz movie, what people publicly portray can often be betrayed by what truly exists in their private lives. A manager brags about his success, but his family is a wreck; a pastor rails against sexual immorality but privately is having an affair; a leader acts as if she has it "all together" but privately feels like a total failure every night. Everyone has a private life and a public life, and there is almost always at least a slight gap between them. But the larger the gap between our public and private lives, the more we have to keep secrets. Secrets require a lot of energy and can sometimes result in a crash if and when people see the chasm between the two images of us. Here are some of the more common things others seldom see but are often at work in our lives and what we can do about them.

Disappointment

Life can be very bruising. Health issues. Financial stress. Work pressures. Family discord. Any one of these can serve as a sobering reminder that things are not turning out the way we had hoped or expected. The result is disappointment. While you may not see it and they may not share it, many of the people you cross paths with every day are feeling it.

Entitlement

Entitlement emerges when we believe we are doing more than others, better than others, or are more valuable than others, and therefore we should be getting more than we are. And you may be surprised by how many of us, deep down and behind the curtain, believe this. This is further fed by comparing ourselves to others in regard to position and pay. If I surround myself with people who tell me how amazing I am or who seem to be advancing faster than I am in life, the roots of entitlement will grow even deeper.

Fear

Fear is a powerful influence in most of our lives. When we are embarrassed or threatened by a person or situation, fear creeps, and sometimes crashes, into our minds. We may not acknowledge it and may even portray the exact opposite – extreme confidence. But behind the curtain, we fear loss – loss of respect, loss of position, loss of health, or loss of money. And it is residing in far more people than just you!

Emotional fragility

Depression, ADHD, anxiety disorders, PTSD, and memory loss are just a few of the emotional issues people may be struggling with behind the curtain. Or they may have a family member struggling which has a challenging impact on his or her life. As humans, we are resilient but also fragile, and no one has unlimited capacity for managing such hardships. We can often "tough it out," continuing to fulfill our basic responsibilities, but behind the curtain are fraying emotions. And one more negative event can result in an emotional crash.

Self-medication

The harder life gets and the more painful it becomes, the greater propensity we have to "treat" ourselves. We write our own prescriptions. Alcohol. Food. Sex. Drugs. Anything that will make us feel better. Disappointment, fear, and entitlement can all feed the medication furnace. Since many people fear the risks of disclosing too much to others, they choose to manage these issues on their own, often via behaviors that will make whatever they are experiencing far worse in the long run. But it will provide a short-term fix of escape and reward or at least pretend to do so.

5 Ways to Manage What Is Behind the Curtain

So, how can leaders manage this? Here are five actions to take.

1. **Remember** – When dealing with others, remember that they all have a life behind the curtain and that life can be very challenging. If all we look at is what we can see in front of us, we will miss divine appointments to help others.

2. **Connect** – The more closely connected you are with those around you, the more you will know what they are dealing with and you can provide emotional support or practical help.

3. **Reflect** – As leaders, we must work to keep the distance between our public lives and private lives close. Remember, the greater the distance,

the greater the secrecy and likelihood for living a compartmentalized, lonely, and even hypocritical life.

4. **Be transparent** – By practicing appropriate transparency with those around us, they see that we too are human, that we too have challenges, and that it is ok to be vulnerable with trustworthy people. Yes, there is risk. But nothing compared to the risk of secrecy and isolation.

5. **Hope** – The message of Jesus is a message of hope. He did not come for the perfect but rather the imperfect. He surrounded himself with flawed people. He offered grace for those feeling judged, forgiveness for those condemned, and hope for those who believe all hope is lost. And hope is the most powerful medicine for life behind the curtain.

The Common Occurrence of Blind Spots & How to Correct Them

Picture yourself with a blindfold on and then attempting to drive a car (bad idea and also illegal!), walk your dog, or throw a Frisbee. It's hard to picture anything but problems emerging. The same is true for those who lead but are unable to see what they should. This results in leading blind, and the outcomes can often be embarrassing at best, and at worst, damaging to ourselves and others.

Like cataracts in the eyes, blind spots often emerge slowly. Sometimes you cannot even tell they are developing until they are fully formed, and by then your sight is limited. Think about the lives of King Saul, leader of Israel, and David, one of his top guys. Saul started his leadership as someone who was known for being humble and valiant. But over time, as David became more successful and popular, Saul became jealous, fearful, and controlling. Saul's blind spots had formed, hardened, and would be difficult to correct. And to point them out to a paranoid king could result in a shorter life expectancy! (More about this drama can be found in the Old Testament book of 1 Samuel, chapters 17-18.)

4 Signs of a Blind Spot

Here are four of the most telling signs of blind spots.

1. People are talking about you but not to you.

"Wow, Bill sure does have bad breath." "Is it me or does Helen dress like it's 1960." "Ever notice how Richard gets angry when someone challenges him?" When people are talking about some of our behaviors that are awkward, embarrassing, or even damaging, that is a sure sign of a blind spot. Most people talk about someone rather than to them because it is easier. Pointing out a blind spot can lead to uncomfortable conversations and even damaged relationships.

2. You have a view of yourself that does not match the majority, but you do not know it.

For example, we have seen many times when an employee believes they are doing not only a good job, but an exceptional one, yet those around them are feeling the opposite. How is that possible? We are all experts at painting a picture of how we see ourselves and then believing that picture is the real thing. But if we could hang that picture next to the ones others would paint of us, they might be very different. Those differences are often our blind spots.

3. You have just enough people that tell you what you need to hear to feel good about yourself.

In recent years, a well-known leader was called out for inappropriate relationships with women who worked for him. The bad behavior was going on for years. And while some of this behavior may have been invisible to others, some of it was very visible, and yet few called him out. It doesn't take many people around a king telling him that he is great, normal, and irreplaceable for him to believe it is true. This situation perpetuates blind spots.

4. Due to loyalty, those closest to you overlook or no longer see your blind spot.

This is why spouses and those closest to us are sometimes the worst at unveiling any shortcomings or embarrassing quirks in our lives. Sometimes, they have been around us so long that they no longer even see them. More often, they don't want to hurt our feelings or run the risk of damaging the relationship. While we all say we are open to and welcome feedback, do we want someone pointing out things like our quirky fear of germs, "unique" style of dress, poor hygiene, or inadequate work ethic?

5 Ways to Manage Blind Spots

So what can a leader do to manage his or her blind spots? Here are five of the best ways to identify and work on your blind spots.

1. Stop living in fantasy land and face it.

Everyone has blind spots including you and me. To ignore this is just further evidence that you have them! Having blind spots exposed can be a bit intimidating. But is the alternative any better? Do you want people talking about you rather than to you?

2. Ask for input.

Ask a simple question to a few people who know you well such as, "What am I doing that I am not aware of but should be?" or "What are the themes of things that people are saying about me rather than to me?"

3. Use tools.

A professionally-designed and anonymous 360 assessment where others give you feedback that is then compared to your self-perception is an excellent way to grow, especially with the help of a skilled coach to guide you. Even a high-quality personality assessment can provide entry into a conversation about blind spots. At The Center Consulting Group, we provide a safe environment to help you identify your blind spots through our Leader 360 Assessment, personality assessment, and experienced coaching.

4. Focus on the important.

Not everything we are oblivious to in our lives is necessary to fix. Focus your energy and attention on those one or two blind spots that may be causing you to lose leadership credibility.

5. Remember that you are not alone.

Every person who can see the gaps in your life also has gaps in their lives that they cannot see. But that is not the issue. We need to first focus on our own blind spots and seek to manage them in such a way as to become a healthier and more effective leader.

10 Reminders for Leaders During a Crisis (& Other Times)

In uncertainty, chaos, and confusion, there are two things we as leaders must do: learn and lead. Here are 10 reminders to help us continue learning and leading well.

1. Leaders spread hope – not fear.

My mom was from a family of 10 children during the Great Depression. She not only survived that, but she also survived World War II, strikes at the steel mill where my dad worked, health scares, the loss of my dad to cancer, and raising three boys (of which I was the easiest ☺). She is now 94 and is a gritty survivor. And we too as leaders should know that we will get through whatever comes as well. It may be hard. There may be losses. And it may never be the same as it was. But we will get through it. We must be the messengers of hope, not fear.

"God is our refuge and strength, an ever-present help in trouble. Therefore we will not fear, though the earth give way and the mountains fall into the heart of the sea, though its waters roar and foam and the mountains quake with their surging." –Psalm 46:1-3

2. Social interaction is not just nice – it is vital.

One of the lessons we have all learned from social distancing due to COVID-19 is that social interaction is as much a vital part of life as are food and medicine. We were created to connect with others. The term "social distancing" may be new for some, but it has been a part of social psychology for many years. And it has often been used in a negative way to describe when a leader keeps people at a social distance so that his or her flaws cannot be seen. Now we have used it to save lives! And people became innovative! People talking to others out of their car window while remaining six feet apart. Neighbors sitting on chairs in the front yard rather than in close quarters. Teams using video conferencing platforms to continue their meetings. Sometimes it takes a crisis to take us back to the basics.

3. Leaders stay focused – keeping everyone's attention on the mission.

While a crisis requires serious attention from leaders and team members, the crisis can also take our sights off of our primary mission – whatever that may be in your organization. When responding to a crisis, it's more important than ever that leaders remind the team (and themselves) about the primary reason of why you are here – serving your clients, members, or customers. Consider how you can turn the crisis into opportunities that will benefit others and help your organization. As someone once said, "Never let a crisis go to waste."

4. The term "innovate or die" will take on new meaning – quickly.

Some nonprofits, churches, and businesses emerge stronger from a crisis. New initiatives will be launched, new services will emerge, new efficiencies will be discovered, and new leaders will surface. In talking with a number of our innovative clients during the initial COVID-19 crisis, they not only were doing scenario planning, they also were mobilizing all of the creative power inside and outside of their organization to fill gaps that did not exist before the crisis. Many innovations, including in medicine as well as other services, emerge only after the pressure is on and the need is deeply felt. You may need to shelter in place, but do not shelter your innovative thinking!

5. Leaders don't have control over everything – but sometimes we think we do.

Why do people look to leaders of all kinds to "fix it"? Because we desperately want to believe that someone can fix it. Leaders have often fed this illusion, and it's also why they sometimes get paid ridiculous amounts of money. But there are cancer cases the doctor can't solve. There are economic disasters the government can't fix. Some viruses cannot be anticipated. Sometimes there are problems beyond the scope of human solutions. Face it – we have limited control. But we will be more likely to get through difficult circumstances when we depend upon help from others and do not try to go solo. Billy Graham once shared this simple yet powerful reminder for those who follow Jesus: "I've read the last page of the Bible. It's all going to turn out all right."

6. Beware of false prophets and self-serving actions – from others and ourselves.

Times of crisis create an ideal environment for the emergence of false prophets and self-serving behavior. False prophets are sometimes obvious – like bad characters trying to take advantage of vulnerable people. But sometimes they are a bit harder to see. For example, after 9/11, the 2008 crash, and now COVID-19, some have tried to position themselves as possessing mysterious knowledge and sophistication in predicting the future. Others only look out for their own interests (like the two guys who drove all over the country buying up hand sanitizer, wipes, and masks in order to take advantage of the COVID-19 crisis). Be wise enough to spot the fool and caring enough to sacrificially serve others.

7. Leaders find solutions – not create anxiety.

Every crisis needs leaders who balance facing reality with solving problems. Anxiety is already an epidemic in our country, so leaders need to reduce it, not compound it. Some leaders forget that people are watching them and listening carefully to what they do say and don't say. We must aim for solutions to a problem and not ramp up anxiety. Years ago, I read a book called *Hard Optimism.* That's a good phrase to define the job description of a leader, especially during times of stress.

"Anyone can hold the helm when the sea is calm."
–Publilius Syrus

8. Leaders communicate – a lot.

We have never heard any leader be accused of over-communicating. Never! During times of uncertainty and crisis, the need for communication is even greater. Communication that joins hope with honesty can calm the nerves and strengthen the spirit of your team. Consider sending daily emails of encouragement or holding regular meetings or video conference calls. And for your customers or clients, regularly check in on them. Depending upon the nature of your business or organization, offer them guidance that will help them navigate these uncertain days. And above all, be a messenger of hope.

"An unreliable messenger stumbles into trouble, but a reliable messenger brings healing." –Proverbs 13:17

9. Weak vital signs increase vulnerability – especially during a crisis.

COVID-19 not only hit our most vulnerable people the hardest, it did the same thing to the most vulnerable organizations. High levels of debt, insufficient cash reserves, outdated products or services, inadequate leadership skills. Over the past decade, there are many organizations, including faith-based ones, that experienced a combination of atrophy and sluggish adaptation to cultural trends. As new enterprises emerge, there will be others that cannot survive either. This serves as a powerful reminder to keep our organizations strong so that we have a greater opportunity to emerge from the devastating blows that are coming now and will come again in the future.

10. Leaders anticipate – crises will happen.

The unexpected is really not that unexpected. Major storms do hit. Economies do crash. Health crises do emerge. Accidents do happen. We should not dwell on but rather anticipate things like: loss of a key employee, loss of a major client, loss of workspace due to a fire, a disruption to your supply chain, a loss of data, etc.

In a crisis, our team can help you manage your communication, plan your next steps, and consider the financial and human implications. We are here for you!

Leaders & Managers: Is There REALLY a Difference?

Quite often, when people talk or write about the differences between leaders and managers, they make it sound as if leaders are first class and managers are, well, somewhere quite a bit below that! In reality, leaders and managers have a lot in common, and sometimes the dichotomy is a bit exaggerated. However, as seen in the following graphic, there are a few things that do differentiate a leader from a manager. Not good versus bad, just different.

There is a lot of gray space between what a leader does and what a manager does as some of their responsibilities can seem similar. However, ALL of the differences listed in the graphic are important to the health and viability of an organization. If an organization gets over-managed and under-led, there will likely be declining innovation. And, if an organization gets over-led and under-managed, there will likely be an unhealthy amount of chaos. A healthy organization needs to be leader-driven and manager-implemented.

MANAGERS VS. LEADERS

MANAGERS...		LEADERS...
Hold a shorter term view	PERSPECTIVE	Hold a longer term view
Centered on a department	RESPONSIBILITY	Centered on the whole organization
Emphasize policies and procedures	PRIORITIES	Emphasize innovation and change
Focus on revenue allocation	REVENUE	Focus on revenue generation
Think tactically	STRATEGY	Think systems

6 Tips to Avoid Leadership Burnout [Hint: Don't Work Less]

Burnout is a term that started being used in the 1970s. While it has never been well-defined, the National Institutes of Health describes it as exhaustion, alienation from work and people, and reduced performance in everyday tasks[6]. Many people attribute burnout to their jobs. But in reality, what is happening at work is only one contributor to stress and burnout. According to the American Psychological Association, money, workplace, and family are the top three contributors. While stress is always going to be a part of life, there are ways to limit or avoid the negative effects of burnout. Here are six tips that can help.

1. Find something you love to do and do more of it.

Leaders often assume they are burning out because of working too many hours. Sometimes this is true, but sometimes it is that leaders are not doing what they are passionate about. If a leader can get to the point of doing 80% of what they love, they will not track hours, they will gain energy. Most leaders don't count hours unless what they are doing is draining, boring, and falling far short of the 80%.

---

6 InformedHealth.org. Cologne, Germany: Institute for Quality and Efficiency in Health Care (IQWiG); 2006-. Depression: What is burnout? [Updated Jun. 18 2020]. www.ncbi.nlm.nih.gov/books/NBK279286/

2. Work with at least one great friend.

When you work with someone you like to be around, the stress of work goes down and the joy of work goes up. This is true even if you have a job you do not like. If you do what you love and get to do it alongside people you love, the likelihood of burnout dramatically goes down. And, if you do not already have at least one great friend at work, nothing is keeping you from developing one!

3. Know yourself and your system.

God has made everyone a bit different. We need to know our bodies and the signs of how we are doing. In addition, we need to know our system which includes our spouse and children and how their uniqueness and expectations influence our energy and health. Some leaders tire out more quickly than others and will need to build endurance. Other leaders may have circumstances in their personal lives that are draining far more energy than their job. You cannot prevent burnout without knowing yourself and your unique circumstances.

4. Leave superman and wonder-woman for the movies.

Sometimes our desire to live up to the expectations of others or our reputation of being "hard workers" and "first in and last out" and "I don't know how she does it all" can place us as leaders in a deadly performance trap. Even when we love what we do and even if we are fortunate enough to work with great friends, we still have limits, and we must monitor and manage those limits or suffer the consequences.

5. Build endurance.

Some leaders need to build more endurance – not reduce stress. In other words, the problem is not that they have too much stress, it is that they do not have a high enough endurance for a leadership role. For these types of leaders, they would do well to have someone coach them in building endurance or grit rather than fleeing from stress. An athlete or soldier does not get stronger by reducing stress but rather by building muscle and endurance over time.

6. Relieve pressure.

There are times that burnout is a real and present danger – declining energy, feeling depressed, lack of motivation, etc. Research is constantly showing that the benefits of exercise can include reducing stress. In addition, be courageous and seek out a medical opinion to see if anything else may be contributing to how you are feeling. Also, consider seeing a counselor or coach for some help in making sense of what you are experiencing. Sometimes, just having a confidential listener can provide enough hope and help you to regain your momentum over time.

Identifying the signs of burnout early and implementing the above tips can help you to avoid it.

Top 5 Reasons People Are Promoted & Fired

If you have ever wondered why others are being promoted ahead of you or why someone was let go from their job, here are the five most common reasons people are promoted and fired. Most of these reasons come from either exceeding or not meeting expectations that your boss has for you. Which side do you lean toward?

Cheating Our Way to the Bottom
5 Ways We Shortchange Ourselves & Others

We all heard about the high-profile case of cheating in the news – wealthy people lying, bribing, and spending huge amounts of money just to get their children into elite universities. It seems pathetic, but they aren't the only ones who cheat. In the TV show Cheaters, people go to the Cheaters Detective Agency when they suspect infidelity from their significant other. Using hidden cameras and surveillance, the Cheaters team investigates the accused and then confronts them when they are caught. What would be discovered if the Cheaters team zeroed in on us as leaders? What would they find? Remember, cheating is not only limited to the high-profile examples we hear about. Here are some of the more common ways we as leaders can shortchange ourselves and others.

Cheating our relationships

We cheat our relationships when we fail to listen to or see the needs of those we claim to care about most. We can miss the practical needs someone has because we are so preoccupied with our busyness and needs. And, we can consistently take far more from our relationships than we give to them. Have you ever felt let down by someone you thought would be there for you – not just during a crisis but also with ongoing friendship, loyalty, and encouragement? If so, you have experienced the bruising that comes from a cheater.

Cheating our future

Most cheating involves directly harming others. However, sometimes we cheat ourselves and don't even know it. The most common way we do this is by failing to invest in our own professional development, thereby hindering our future potential and even income. Another common way we cheat ourselves is by failing to plan for the financial future of ourselves and our families – when we don't seek professional financial guidance or when we fail to delay the vacation or car purchase this year to be better prepared for five years from now.

Cheating our family

We can cheat our families or significant others in multiple ways. First, we can work so much that we don't have any time to invest in them and just be with them – like the parents who neglect to nurture their child's spiritual and character development or the child who seldom has mom or dad show up at their sporting or musical events. Or second, we can work too little and fail to provide adequately for their financial needs – like the parents who intentionally choose to not work harder or invest in their career, passing over opportunities that would have allowed them to assist their children who are now in massive debt for education. We can also cheat our children by doing everything for them and not allowing them to develop on their own – like the example of high-profile parents using bribery to get their children into elite universities. All of these families have been cheated.

Cheating our employer

When we think of cheating an employer, we normally think of "really bad" things like embezzlement. But most employees don't steal money from where they work, at least not directly. However, a lot of passive stealing takes place that results in the same long-term outcome – not doing the right thing on behalf of our employer. One way this happens is by not staying engaged in our job or the organization's mission. Another example is using our time in ways that do not contribute to productive results such as excessive time on Facebook, Twitter, or internet shopping. These actions (or inactions) result in companies losing billions of dollars each year. That's why it's called cheating!

Cheating God

Cheating God sounds pretty bad. But, in reality, we cheat God regularly. All of the previous points are cheating God in some form. And when we cheat God, we also cheat ourselves. One way we cheat God is when we neglect to listen to him and what he has to say about our lives (this is called pride). Another way is when we allow people or things to edge God out of his VIP seat in our lives (this is called idolatry). We also cheat him when we get too lazy or too busy to make room for him in our lives (this is called being lukewarm). We may not completely disconnect from God, we just make him a peer to the many other things we deem important, cheating him out of his premier role. However we do it, the result is the same: God gets cheated.

So, what can a cheater do?

It's great when we can quit cheating habits cold turkey. But, sometimes that can be hard to do. Here are a few suggestions on how to stop cheating yourself and those around you:

1. Identify where your cheating is causing the most harm and go after it.

2. Start somewhere. When it comes to bad behavior, any improvement is better than none.

3. Ask yourself, "What short-term benefit am I getting from my cheating, and why do I believe that benefit is so important?"

4. Have someone help you since changing bad behavior is hard to do alone.

5. When you fail, and you will, don't quit. Cheating is hard to overcome but it is not impossible.

"Whoever walks in integrity walks securely, but whoever takes crooked paths will be found out." - Proverbs 10:9

Trust: The Element of Leadership You Cannot Afford to Ignore

Did you know . . .

- Employees in high trust environments have 50% higher productivity and 74% less stress. ("The Neuroscience of Trust" by Paul Zak. *Harvard Business Review,* 2017)

- Only 46% of employees place "a great deal of trust" in their employers. ("A Global Survey on the Ambiguous State of Employee Trust" by Karyn Twaronite. *Harvard Business Review,* 2016)

- 55% of CEOs believe that a lack of trust is a threat to their organization's growth. (*19th Annual Global CEO Survey* by PwC, January 2016)

With all of the research, articles, books, and TED talks about trust, you would expect a great new discovery to have emerged! But in reality, the principles of trust have remained the same from generation to generation – even children learn at a young age the importance of trust and what results when someone violates their trust. Just watch a child's response when he is not included in a game that all of his "friends" are playing and the betrayal that follows! Why the hurt and betrayal? Because the child trusted his friends to include him, and the friends did not live up to that expectation.

Trust is the confidence that a person or organization is credible and will live up to our expectations. We know that trust is foundational to all of society. For example, just think about what your life would look like if you had to verify EVERYTHING. The sources of your food. The sterilization process used at your dentist. Where your kids are at every hour. The credentials of your doctor. The background of your neighbors. The motives of your boss! You get the point. It is not that verifying someone's credentials or checking on the veracity of an institution with which you do business is wrong. It just takes time, and if we tried to verify everyone with whom we are connected or every institution with which we intersect, we would have time for nothing else since trust is foundational to all of life and society. So, if trust is so essential both personally and professionally, how do we most often damage it?

Top 3 Ways to Lose Trust

While there are many ways to damage trust, here are the top three ways that will strip it the fastest.

1. Be soft on honesty

It is stating the obvious to say that blatant lies and deception will result in decreased trust in the person who is being untruthful. But for most leaders, it is not the outright lies that get them in trouble – it is the massaging or "varnishing" of the truth that causes people to wonder if what you say is an accurate representation or description. Overstating, underreporting, giving different descriptions to different people… you get the picture. When we are soft on honesty, we are stripping people's trust in us.

2. Be hard on others

It is one thing to challenge people to stretch and grow in their effectiveness. Coaches do this daily in the lives of athletes. However, it is a completely different thing to be hard on others. When I refer to someone being hard on others, I am referring to them being constantly critical, harsh, uncaring, and even toxic. We may trust someone who pushes us to be better and move beyond what is comfortable, but it would be strange and unhealthy to trust and want to work for someone who makes us feel defeated, worthless, or even worse – threatened. When we are hard on others, we will lose some or possibly all of the trust people may have in us.

3. Be arrogant

You know an arrogant person when you meet one. They know better than everyone else. They believe they are special and want to be treated that way. They take the credit for the successes and shift the blame for the mistakes. They expect a seat at the C-suite table because they believe they are entitled to it. And, they are not at all interested in transparency and vulnerability. Why? Because to do so would result in a scene similar to the Wizard of Oz – when the curtain is pulled back, all there was to see was an embarrassed, insecure little man! When we manifest arrogance, we elevate ourselves and suppress others which will only serve to kill trust.

7 Behaviors that Build Trust

So what are some of the most important behaviors to fuel trust? Here are seven to consider.

1. Be consistent

When we are consistent in our emotions and performance, people are more likely to trust us. Unpredictable mood swings and inconsistent performance in our work will cause people to trust us less.

2. Be personable

It is actually quite simple – people tend to give the benefit of the doubt to others who are warm and friendly. This is why those with emotional intelligence often exceed those who just have intellectual intelligence in long-term career success.

3. Be competent

Would you go to a surgeon who has a reputation of being rated as a solid C minus? It is unlikely. We are more likely to trust others who are highly competent. The same is true for us as leaders – people will be more inclined to follow us when they are confident that we are good at our jobs.

4. Be honest

People tend to trust those they deem to be truthful; this is obvious. And this is also why the damage is so serious when a person we granted our trust to violates it by lying to us or varnishing the truth. We want to believe in others, and we are greatly disappointed when they deceive us.

5. Be caring

When we show genuine interest in and concern for others, they are far more likely to trust us. Why would you trust someone who is cold, uncaring, and shows no interest in you? Although there are those rare times when all you need is a short-term (yet vital) need to be met - like a patient with a specialist physician.

6. Be open

Appropriate transparency with organizational information as well as vulnerability about yourself as a person and leader helps others see that you trust them enough to share. Being open and admitting mistakes models transparency which deepens the trust between you and others.

7. Be a promoter

Not of yourself but of others. There are few things more pathetic than when a leader or manager limits the growth or success of others, often due to his or her own insecurities. When we look out for the interest of others by helping them advance and succeed and by recognizing their contributions, we cultivate seeds of trust.

If you want to experience long term success, healthy teams, improved relationships, and more productive workplaces, focus on the trust factor. Trust is the most effective gauge to monitor on your leadership dashboard.

7 Life Principles That Will Not Let You Down

One word that we hear a lot from leaders today is BUSY. It is this sense of busyness and stress that often hinders us from reading and the pursuit of learning. The following are seven life principles, one for each day of the week. It will only require about three minutes each day to read the principle and apply it to your life and leadership. Even while managing the busyness of life, it is important to keep growing and learning!

Day 1: Guard Yourself.

"Above all else, guard your heart, for everything you do flows from it." Proverbs 4:23

Temptations and traps are common to all people. But leaders have some that are especially unique to them. Power. Control. Entitlement. Prestige. These, combined with the age-old ones of money and sex, make leaders vulnerable. It is for this reason that we are charged to guard our hearts above all else.

Day 2: Strive for Peace.

"If it is possible, as far as it depends on you, live at peace with everyone." Romans 12:18

Your workplace. Your family. Your neighborhood. Do whatever is in your control to live at peace with others. Most feel painful levels of stress in the midst of conflict. Others feed off of strife. While conflict is not always avoidable, we should make every effort to strive for peace in our relationships. Yes, there are times when peace is not possible. But perhaps there are times when we are more interested in winning than in relating well.

Day 3: Help Others.

"...not looking to your own interests but each of you to the interests of others." Philippians 2:4

It is natural to look out for ourselves. No training required, right? But it is unnatural to intentionally and consistently look out for the interests of others. This is called servanthood. Helping others grow, get ahead, solve a problem, get a raise, or even just asking about their lives are a few of the practical ways we can help others.

Day 4: Speak Truth.

"Instead, speaking the truth in love..." Ephesians 4:15

Ephesians 4:15 is a commonly quoted verse from the Bible – Speak the truth in love. Some of us are much better at one part than the other – offering a lot of "nice" but not so much "truth" while others offer a lot of "truth" but are a bit short on the "nice." But nothing can wreck our credibility faster than failing to speak what we feel to be true regarding our perspective on a situation or decision. If you genuinely want to help others, speak truth – but in a respectful and genuinely caring way.

Day 5: Pursue Wisdom.

"...turning your ear to wisdom and applying your heart to understanding..." Proverbs 2:2

Have you seen the bumper sticker that says "Warning: I do stupid things"? Amazing that we brag about it by putting it in writing on our car! Perhaps we all should own one since we all do stupid things somewhere along the path of life. But there is a difference between a mistake and a pattern of doing dumb things. If we are serious about making smart choices, we must pursue wisdom. Seek out advice. Surround yourself with wise people. Do whatever you must to not do stupid things!

Day 6: Answer Gently.

"A gentle answer turns away wrath, but a harsh word stirs up anger." Proverbs 15:1

Gruff. Abrupt. Sarcastic. Rude. Condescending. Aggressive. These are just a few of the opposites of "gentle." And I can honestly say that I am too gifted in at least one of them. Sometimes we can associate gentleness with being feminine. But it has nothing to do with gender, and instead has to do with respect. Will I choose to respect someone enough to talk to them in a manner and tone that displays respect? Aggressiveness is often returned with aggressiveness. But gentleness disarms and often results in a better outcome than an unhealthy escalation.

Day 7: Be Courageous.

"Have I not commanded you? Be strong and courageous. Do not be afraid; do not be discouraged..." Joshua 1:9

People can be courageously stupid. Smart courage is built upon seeking wise counsel and pursuing wisdom. There is a reason the Bible says on multiple occasions to be strong and courageous and to not be afraid and discouraged. Leaders will face hard decisions, ones that will make some people very unhappy. Leaders must be courageous enough to make those decisions but to do so with humility and gentleness rather than arrogance and harshness.

How the Mighty Fall: 6 Ways We Can Self-Destruct & Not Know It

Over the past few years, there have been multiple high-profile stories in the news of influential people who have fallen off or been knocked down from the pedestals of power and prestige. From sports and Hollywood to business and politics, and even to education and religion. Here are the most common ways we can self-destruct and not even know it.

1. Arrogance

Our success can build up a residue of arrogance, but not in a way that we can see it in ourselves. After all, because we are so successful, we know we are not arrogant – we are just right!

2. Invincibility

The more successful we become and the more that goes right for us, the more we believe that we are untouchable. This is often affirmed by those around us who lead us to believe we are irreplaceable.

3. Entitlement

We are the reason for all of the success around us, so why are we not entitled to more money, special treatment, and favors? And as we grow in our success, we often associate with other "successful" people and see what they have, further breeding the belief that we too are entitled to the same.

4. Collusion

When the people around us are getting some form of benefit from us, they can fail to tell us anything that may cause those benefits to go away – even if they have concerns. We give them what they want from us, and they tell us what we want and need to hear.

5. Contamination

Those of us at the top of an organization create the culture within it. The more we become arrogant, invincible, and entitled, the more we will embed these dysfunctions in our teams and overall organizational culture. In other words – we contaminate the worksite!

6. Denial

It's fascinating how delusional and hardened we can become as leaders, even when confronted with evidence of our failures and flaws. A spirit of arrogance and people telling us we are "fantastic" can build up a high and thick wall of denial regarding our human weaknesses.

As leaders, we would all do well to have at least a few truth-tellers in our lives – people who will not back down or shy away from serving as a mirror for us. And, it may also be beneficial to tape this proverb on our computer screen and read it multiple times each day:

"When pride comes, then comes disgrace, but with humility comes wisdom." -Proverbs 11:2

How to Handle Confrontation with Compassionate Candor

"Shoot straight." "Tell it like it is." "Be honest." These are just a few of the phrases we often hear when it comes to candor. To speak to someone with candor is to speak with forthrightness. But it is easier said than done. People tend to either be so blunt that they do not reflect any compassion or so compassionate that they withhold vital input. And, have you ever noticed how those who cry out the most about the importance of candor in their organization or team like to give it but do not like it when others are forthright with them? Candor sounds great until it comes your way.

Caring vs. Confronting

Our goals as leaders, managers, and friends should be compassionate candor – speaking to others in a way that is both forthright AND caring; this can also be referred to as "Constructive Engagement." Remember that not everything we see in someone needs to be addressed. That would make me even more annoying than I already am! But behaviors or shortcomings that can cause harm to ourselves, to our organizations, or to others need constructive engagement.

Look at the following chart. Where do you fall? Where would others place you? Where would you place these well-known TV characters?

- Sheldon Cooper - *The Big Bang Theory*

- Robert Herjavec - *Shark Tank*
- Mr. Rogers - *Mister Rogers' Neighborhood*
- Marie Baron - *Everybody Loves Raymond*

Why is compassionate candor not more common? The primary answer is FEAR. Fear of losing a relationship, fear of losing a job or opportunity for advancement, and fear of the stress and awkwardness that come with being forthright.

Remember this: when considering candor, people tend to over-estimate the potential for bad outcomes and under-estimate the potential for good outcomes.

How to move towards Compassionate Candor

If you are on the giving end of Compassionate Candor:

1. Know yourself: Which quadrant am I normally in and why?

2. Ask yourself: What is the issue, and is it important enough or necessary?

3. Prepare yourself: balance care and confrontation by being...

   Direct: Talk directly to the person rather than talking to everyone else about him or her.

   Specific: Give examples or illustrations that would help the person better understand what you are talking about and why it is important.

   Non-punishing: Use language and tone that is adequate enough for them to hear you in light of his or her unique personality, but do not be damaging or toxic. As a general rule, if you are angry, wait.

And if you are on the receiving end of Compassionate Candor:

1. Defensiveness is normal, so be aware and manage it.

2. Be humble enough to listen respectfully.

3. Seek feedback BEFORE it comes to you unsolicited.

Not All That Spreads Is Bad: 6 Things That Spread Positivity

Corona, Ebola, Swine, Avian. Viruses spread and leave emotional, physical, and economic fallout. But not everything that spreads is bad. For example, some viruses help protect us. We have viruses residing in our bodies that attack invaders! Leaders can also spread both bad and good things that will affect their organizations. Here are six good things that can be spread and have a positive effect.

Laughter

In our consulting practice, we have found a positive correlation between teams that laugh together and the overall health of the organization. When we interact with groups and do not hear them laugh and joke with one another, we start to look a bit deeper. Why? Because laughter is a sign of health and is also contagious.

Encouraging words

Have you ever heard the phrase, "Hurt people hurt others"? Often, we can say the same thing about encouragement. "Encouraged people encourage others." Many people go through life feeling beat down, taken advantage of, and having an overabundance of self-doubt. The spread of genuine encouragement can make the difference between a very hard day and a very good day. Choose to make someone's day good.

Purpose

Laugher and encouragement feel intuitive regarding how they spread. But purpose? How do we spread that? As leaders, purpose is the one thing we MUST spread. Leaders do this by helping others see how their role, regardless of how small or hidden, matters to the overall vision and values of your organization. God created us for purposeful work. So, consider spreading some purpose today.

Optimism

How many people say, "I want to work with a negative person"? Or, "I just feel so good after spending time with him; he sees all that is wrong with me and the world"? The line is very short for those who respond well to pessimism. But not all kinds of optimism are beneficial either. There is blind optimism, this is not recommended since it is as destructive as pessimism, and healthy optimism, not ignoring reality but still choosing hope. In our coaching and consulting work, we have seen over and over that both optimism and pessimism spread easily. Choose carefully.

Recognition

The U.S. Department of Labor once noted that the number one reason people leave a job is that they do not feel appreciated[7]. While some people have an insatiable need for being recognized, most just appreciate periodically hearing a well-earned praise or thank you. When we recognize someone, they feel encouraged, become more

---

7 Tom Rath and Donald O. Clifton, *How Full Is Your Bucket?: Positive Strategies for Work and Life* (New York: Gallup Press, 2009).

optimistic, and tend to be more positive around others. That's called spreading health.

Helpfulness

In their book, *How Full is Your Bucket,* authors Tom Rath and Donald Clifton tell the story about studying 4,583 call center representatives from one company. They found three specific employees who turned off EVERY customer with whom they came in contact! (I think somewhere along the way I would have talked with each of those employees.) But they also found seven who retained every customer they served. That is the difference helpfulness can make.

In seasons of anxiety and heightened awareness, consider how you as a leader can spread these six things that will produce positive and lasting results.

7 Insecurities That Can Hold Good Leaders Back

When was the last time you heard yourself or another leader acknowledge being insecure? Almost never, right? Yet, every leader has some insecurities, if they aren't too insecure to acknowledge them. A tinge of jealousy. A sense of doubt. A hint of fear. A lack of confidence. Insecurities are often surfaced when someone else is complimented, given recognition, or promoted. We may ignore them or deny them, but insecurities are there, and when left unmanaged, they can damage our relationships, our credibility, and even harm the organizations we lead. Here are seven of the most common insecurities that can hold good leaders back.

1. Someone is more innovative than me.
Sign of insecurity: Striving to take credit for the success of the team or others.

2. Someone is more networked than me.
Sign of insecurity: Letting people know you are a "player" by dropping names of who you know.

3. Someone is liked more than me.
Sign of insecurity: Trying extra hard to be "liked" rather than to be "respected."

4. Someone is smarter than me.
Sign of insecurity: Attempting to look like an expert in every area of life and leadership.

5. Someone is outpacing me.
Sign of insecurity: Sabotaging them by either holding them back or by criticizing them.

6. Someone is better looking than me.
Sign of insecurity: Blaming their looks for their success instead of their skills.

7. Someone is younger than me.
Sign of insecurity: Using their age as a weapon against them.

What should you do if any of these insecurities ring true for you? First, it's ok to acknowledge it for what it is. Every leader has experienced feelings of insecurity at some point. And those who say they never have are too insecure to acknowledge it! When you experience insecurity, ask yourself, "Why?" "Why am I threatened?" "Why am I anxious?" "Why am I jealous?" Often, triggers of insecurity grow out of not feeling valued or good enough. If you find yourself being hindered by this, a good coach or counselor may be able to help guide you through it.

"We all have self-doubt. You don't deny it, but you also don't capitulate to it." —Kobe Bryant

Critical Thinker vs. Critical Person

The difference between a person who thinks critically and a person who is critical is subtle yet drastic. The following explains how you can tell the difference and how you can adjust your actions to be a critical thinker.

WHICH ARE YOU?

CRITICAL THINKER VS. CRITICAL PERSON

Critical Thinker	Critical Person
Asks questions to learn	Asks questions to embarrass
Looks at things from different perspectives	Looks at things from one perspective – their own!
Contributes to solutions	Contributes to problems
Generates ideas	Critiques ideas
Rewards risk-taking and experimentation	Hinders risk-taking and experimentation
Welcomes questions of their ideas	Questions others but does not like being questioned
Contributes to hope and innovation	Contributes to fear and low morale

How to Vaccinate Your Organization From Dysfunction & Decline

We have vaccinations for the flu, pneumonia, shingles, and a host of other health woes. Wouldn't it be great if we could vaccinate our organizations against painful and sometimes deadly outcomes? Here are six actions to take to vaccinate your organization against decline.

1. Find wise counsel and listen to it.

The book of Proverbs found in the Bible refers to the importance of wisdom and wise counsel many times. If you want to protect yourself and your organization, ensure you have people who can provide wisdom to you and then make sure you listen to it! Team members already on your team, peer groups, and professional consultants can all add value in providing wise counsel.

2. Recruit talent and retain it.

If you want to protect your organization from decline, it will require finding and keeping the best people. There is often a supply shortage of the talent needed by many organizations. Talented employees are hard to find, and it requires intentional effort to retain them. Remember, talent attracts talent. The healthier and more effective you are as a leader, the more likely you are to attract talent.

3. Build and guard cash reserves.

Churches, businesses, and nonprofits have at least one thing in common – they often do not have enough cash reserves to endure a lengthy crisis. To vaccinate your organization, build cash reserves and then guard those reserves from the many ideas and hands that will try to withdraw from them. Withdrawals may be needed one day, but they better be for good reason.

4. Take a risk but test it.

You may think that in order to guard against decline you should avoid risk. Wrong! Not taking risks is a surefire way to set your organization on the path of slow but sure decline. To ensure your organization does not enter into decline, you need to continually learn of the emerging trends, potential disruptions, and unique opportunities that could meet your needs – but test the idea before investing everything into it. In other words, beta-test it!

5. Change out people who don't fit.

One of the hardest decisions leaders have to make is to transition out a person who is not a fit for the position, is not a fit for the organization's culture, or does not possess the level of skill that is now needed. However, if you have invested in the person's success and their performance is still not good enough, avoiding the change will put your organization at risk and can even put the individual at risk by having to change him or her out later and older.

6. Look accurately at yourself and deal with it.

Last, but not least, we need to look at ourselves as leaders and determine if we are leading at the level that is needed. Are we a source of health, vision, and inspiration in our team and organization? Or increasingly a source of irritation, insecurity, and control? If you want to vaccinate your organization from decline, the first step may be to take a look in the mirror and ask yourself, "Why would anyone want to be led by me?"

15 Disciplines That Will Strengthen Your EQ

I have never heard of a person failing or being held back because he or she was too emotionally intelligent! But I have watched many fail or not reach their potential because they were bordering on clueless when it came to relating to others. There are a variety of great books and articles on the topic of emotional intelligence (EQ), but sometimes practical suggestions are in short supply. Here are 15 disciplines each of us can use to strengthen our emotional and relational intelligence.

1. Initiate a meal

Enjoy a meal with someone different than your normal network at least one day each week. You are never too busy to do this once per week! And, meals often have a way of setting people at ease.

2. Ask questions

Practice asking at least two questions of every person you meet. Questions show interest and may include their weekend activities, family, special events, or important projects.

3. Pursue connection

Seek time with those above you and those below you in the organizational hierarchy. It's most natural to spend time with peers. Break it up and initiate time with supervisors and subordinates as well as people in departments unrelated to yours.

4. Watch others

Identify one or two people who are great relaters and learn. This is a great way to strengthen your EQ. You should not try to be just like them, but you can learn what they do well and what would fit with who you are.

5. Ask for feedback

Find a few trusted and truthful friends and periodically ask them for feedback on your relational style. We cannot grow or learn about much of anything, including emotional intelligence, without input from other sources.

6. Be transparent

Transparency helps form stronger emotional connections to others. However, transparency requires discernment since sharing too much personal information or asking too personal of a question with someone you only know casually can reflect poor emotional intelligence rather than build it!

7. Read

Select a good book or a few articles on building emotional and relational strength. Dr. Travis Bradberry and Dr. Daniel Goleman are just a few writers worth reading on the topic of emotional intelligence along with Dr. David Marks' article "Making Relational Glue" found in The Center Consulting Group's book *FIT – Improving the Leadership Health of Yourself and Others.*

8. Affirm

Intentionally find a way to offer affirmation to each person with whom you interact. Affirmation, when genuine, can build trust and a relational bond with others.

9. Plan

For some people, it is helpful to think about the person and conversation in advance of having it. This is especially true if you do not feel confident in your management of emotional and relational interactions.

10. Send a note or email

Taking the time to send a positive note to someone reinforces your attention to strengthening your EQ, and the person will appreciate it. Some people find they can express themselves better in writing than in a face-to-face meeting, and people find encouraging notes to be... encouraging!

11. Monitor intensity and tone

People who are good at building vibrant relationships pay attention to how they are speaking, the volume at which they are speaking, and the body language they are manifesting when they are speaking.

12. Smile more

Yes, something as simple as a smile can make us more inviting and less intimidating. This is another reminder that our non-verbal language is as powerful as what we say with words.

13. Focus

Focus, but not on your phone or on the surrounding distractions! Focus on the person in front of you and do everything within your power to not lose that focus. Eliminate as many distractions as possible.

14. Walk around

Sitting too long at your desk is not only not physically healthy, it is also not relationally healthy. Intentionally walk around to other offices to say hi, check in on how people are doing, and let them know you are interested in more than just the tasks at hand.

15. Reconcile quickly

Conflict is natural and often necessary to form healthy relationships. But left unresolved, feelings can fester and relational infection can set in causing long-term harm.

Start implementing one or two of these disciplines each week to help strengthen emotional and relational intelligence!

10 Things Deceptive Leaders Do to Fake Their Way to Success

"There is nothing new under the sun." This well-known phrase found in the Bible was written thousands of years ago and yet accurately captures the nature of human behavior today. I was reminded of it after reading the book *Bad Blood* by John Carreyrou which is about Theranos, the fast-to-rise and fast-to-collapse blood-testing company. Thinking about this company and its leaders reminded me of many other deceptive leaders like Bernie Madoff (leader of the largest financial fraud case in U.S. history) and Jack Bennett, founder of the Foundation for New Era Philanthropy (a Ponzi scheme that negatively impacted 1,100 individuals, churches, and nonprofits). While most deceptive leaders do not become as infamous as Bernie Madoff, they do have some things in common in faking their way to success.

1. Making visionary promises.

Deceptive leaders are often visionaries, and vision is a good thing... when it can be accomplished. In the case of Theranos, who wouldn't want to have their blood tested with a simple prick of the finger and have the results within hours rather than days? However, deceptive leaders are notorious for making grandiose promises that have a ring of truth yet cannot be delivered either at all or to the level at which they had advertised.

2. Varnishing the truth.

While there are many examples of unhealthy leaders outright lying, many start with a little varnishing of the truth. Varnished truth is when you take something that has some factual aspect and then place a coating of mistruth over it either through exaggeration, misrepresentation, or only partial disclosure of the truth.

3. Creating a sense of mystery.

From the classified security details of the small mysterious testing unit of Theranos to the secret donors providing the matching funds for New Era, surrounding each was a sense of mystery. Deceptive leaders are uniquely skilled at creating an environment full of mystery. And people are attracted to magic even though they know it does not exist.

4. Attracting highly credible sponsors.

One tactic of unhealthy leaders is to ensure a smell of legitimacy regarding their promises by recruiting credible people to endorse their products or services. New Era had the endorsement of John Templeton and highly respected institutions such as the University of Pennsylvania. Theranos had former Secretaries of State Henry Kissinger and George Schultz. This tactic causes others to feel safe by believing "this many smart people can't be wrong."

5. Punishing those who question.

"You want to know more than what is being shared? OK – then you will not get funding from New Era." "You question our ethics of what is being done with blood tests? Fine – you are fired for lack of loyalty." Deceptive leaders are like snipers. They pick off one person at a time who they deem to be damaging or dangerous to their deception. In short, they don't like being questioned, and they like being told "no" even less.

6. Telling bold lies and maybe even believing them.

Some deceptive leaders are blatant in their deception – they are lying, and they know they are lying. Others appear to live in a confused space somewhere between "I am only trying to help others" and "I am a narcissistic sociopath who cannot tell the difference between truth and deception." What is amazing is that, even when they are caught and the truth is piled to the ceiling, they will still try to work their magic!

7. Influencing others to suspend normal judgment.

How is it that very smart people can follow pathological leaders? In most cases, they have to convince themselves to suspend normal judgment. Those investing in Madoff's scheme or with New Era knew they were getting far better than normal returns. But when suspicion would surface, they could always say, "Even though I do not understand it, I trust so and so, and I know they would never embrace something that is not right or true."

8. Creating a demand for access.

When people see others benefiting from the magic that is being worked by deceptive leaders, they fear that they are missing out. Investors see others making great returns and are told "he doesn't accept too many clients." Nonprofits see others getting big checks and desperately want in on the action and are told, "You have to be invited in." And the longer this goes on, the more outsiders want to get in on the deal.

9. Keeping experts at a distance.

Deceptive leaders often succeed by working to be the smartest one in the room. How do they do it? By keeping people smarter than themselves away. Think about this, Theranos was a bio-medical company, and yet it did not have any experts in blood science on its board nor did most biotech venture capital groups invest in it. They did have a lot of expert researchers working for them, and their board was made up of very intelligent individuals. However, the expert researchers were not allowed to have all of the details, and therefore their expertise was relegated to one small part of the big picture.

10. Controlling information.

Deceptive leaders are very skilled at controlling information, including who knows what and how much they are allowed to know. Bernie Madoff accomplished this by having a very small and loyal staff that included many family members. To control information at Theranos, Elizabeth Holmes used lawyers and I.T. staff and prevented staff from sharing information with each other. Accurate information is power, and those who have access to all of the information have all of the power.

What is fascinating about these cases is how such large and elaborate illusions were exposed by a rather small collection of less powerful people who triggered the alarm. Theranos was exposed by a few courageous employees and a rather obscure pathologist blogger. New Era's curtain of deception was pulled back from an accounting professor from a small college. And Bernie Madoff's sons exposed his bogus business.

We all would do well to make the same request found in Psalm 120:2, "Deliver me, O Lord, from lying lips, from a deceitful tongue." And this includes not only delivering us from the damaging effects of the deception of others but also protecting us from ourselves.

How to Get More Done, Empower Others & Guard Against Overload

I once read a crazy, yet funny story of an event in China. One businessman wanted to kill another, so he hired a hitman. But instead of doing the job, that hitman hired another, paying him a portion of what he received and keeping the rest. But instead of doing the hit, the second guy hired a third hitman and paid him an even lower amount to do the job. Then the third hitman did the same thing again. In all, the murder was passed on to another hitman five times. And in the end, the fifth guy did not even do it – he told the guy he was supposed to kill and they told the police! Let's just say, that was a very poor example of delegation.

Delegation is the art of empowering others to do what they are capable of doing so that you can do more of what only you can do. And it is an art. Throughout a leader's career, almost all will struggle with either not delegating ("there is no one experienced enough to do it right") or delegating poorly ("I don't feel like doing it, so I'll just give it to her"). Here are 10 practical steps to advancing your organization's effectiveness by wise delegation.

10 Steps to Delegation

1. Hire people who are trustworthy and train them to the point that you have confidence in them. If you ever lack confidence in a staff member to whom you should be delegating, ask yourself, why? Did you hire the right person? Did you provide them training and

opportunities to develop the knowledge and skills? Did you give them a chance to prove themselves? Did you give them coaching if they were failing?

2. Identify five tasks or projects you should not be doing but are important enough to be done. Delegation is not only about which tasks to give away, it is also about which ones to keep! And remember, not everything should be delegated, and delegation is NOT a way to give you more time to play, loaf, or be lazy! It should give you more time to add value to your organization's vision and your leadership health and effectiveness.

3. Identify the best people you have to do each of the designated projects or tasks. If you feel you have no one, it is a sign that you have not succeeded at Step 1! Go back to Step 1 and accomplish it.

4. Provide your employee with clear explanations, expectations, and authority regarding the project or task. What do you want? When do you want it? What parameters or boundaries must they follow? Delegation often fails because the expectations were not clear on the front end. Now, let go, and let them lead! Ask them if they are confident in being successful with the task, and if not, what it will take to become confident.

5. Provide them with regular accountability and feedback. This type of regular monitoring is done by communicating your expectations for project

updates and completion dates. No deadline often means no completion! Also, give feedback on how they are doing and agree to which communication methods you prefer for staying informed.

6. Do not allow the task to be given back to you! Sometimes people like to practice "reverse delegation." Reverse delegation is when you ultimately end up with the task back in your bin. Do not allow that to happen. Your employee needs to walk away with the project, and the project needs to remain with them, not you. Remember, only jump back in when absolutely necessary.

7. Trust them to be successful. Provide encouragement and support to let them know that you are confident in them. Sometimes we can unintentionally send a message of doubt that causes people to live up to our lack of trust by losing confidence in themselves and failing. In other words, don't interfere without a very good reason.

8. Don't expect the task to be done exactly the same way you would do it. This is not realistic and does not leave room for the task to be done in perhaps an even better way. However, it is realistic to expect that it be done to a reasonable standard and that standard should have been clearly defined in Step 4.

9. If you feel they are not succeeding, test your assumptions. Meet with them for an update. Determine if you communicated clear expectations

and provided them with the resources to do it successfully. Also determine if your expectations regarding the timing, deliverables, and methods are realistic. Do not take the task back, but rather coach them to do it again and to succeed.

10. Celebrate success with them by giving both private and public recognition. Such acknowledgment will build their confidence for future projects. People pay attention to what leaders recognize and celebrate.

The long-term success of a leader and long term growth of an organization will be tied to how well a leader delegates.

"When you delegate tasks, you create followers. When you delegate authority, you create leaders."
– Craig Groeschel, founder of Life Church

The 6 Greatest Fears Leaders Face & What to Do About Them

Regardless of what you hear, fear is a powerful motivator. God gives us the ability to detect danger and respond accordingly. The same is true in leadership. While many leaders try to portray themselves as fearless, they are mere mortals with fears common to us all. And, what we fear most can ultimately begin to rule us. Here are six of the most common fears leaders face.

1. Loss of Control

Leaders like control. Period. That is not necessarily a bad thing unless the control is more for the benefit of the leader rather than to advance the mission. Would you want to go into surgery wondering if the surgeon has control of the room?! But when leaders hoard control and fear losing it, it can often result in bad outcomes. I remember hearing of a leader who told his team, "This is my meeting and my organization!" Which translates to, "I am fearful of losing my control."

2. Irrelevance

If you watch any great athletic event such as the Olympics or Superbowl, they always show or interview the celebrities of the past. It cannot be easy knowing that they were once the stars that everyone wanted to know, and now many from the next generation do not even know (or care) who they are. It is this type of irrelevance that can create a lot of fear in leaders, especially as they get older. The fear of "no one really cares about what I think."

3. Getting Older

Ok, I confess that I am getting annoyed with my body increasingly not listening to my instructions. Every time I look up my new symptoms on WebMD (I really shouldn't do this, I know), it tells me that smoking, drinking, and being overweight can contribute to the problem I am experiencing. But I do not drink, I do not smoke, and I am not overweight! The real problem is that I am getting older and my body doesn't act as I wish. And it is likely yours does not either – even if you are not "old." Getting older is both a state of body and of mind, and if we are not careful, it can dominate our thoughts and our leadership.

4. Failure

The fear of failure is similar to the fear of losing control but with its own complexities. Whether you are 25 or 55, the fear of failing can be an all-consuming preoccupation. It can influence us to not take risks if we do not have a backup security plan. When there is a failure, a leader's fear may cause him or her to blame others rather than to own it. While fear can be a valuable ally to a leader, serving as a warning system of potential danger, it can also cause a leader to play it safe, sit on the sidelines, and coast.

5. Not Getting the Credit

Have you ever sat in a meeting and watched someone else get some or all of the credit for an idea that you generated? Your inner voice starts to say, "Are you going to let them get away with that? Speak up! Tell them it was YOU." This is called fear of not getting the credit. It is real. It is common. And it is human. After all, there is nothing wrong with wanting credit for something you did or created. That is why we have trademark and copyright laws. But *who* gets the credit should always be subservient to *is the mission being advanced.*

6. Someone Better or Smarter

Everyone has competed in either sports, academics, or career. You finally arrive at a place on the team or a position in the company, and you are feeling good. Confident. Successful. That is until HE or SHE shows up. That person who is a little (or a lot) better or smarter than you. It is common, and often creates insecurity and fear that you may lose your place. The compliments and commendations you once received diminish, and the other person is now the recipient. That reaction you start to get in your brain when this happens – it is called fear.

3 Things to Focus on When Facing Our Fear

While fear is normal, it does not serve us well if it dominates our thoughts and becomes the driving force behind most of our actions. There will always be someone better, faster, smarter, or even younger right behind you. So rather than focusing on that, focus on these three things to help you face your fear.

1. First, it is important to remind yourself that you are not alone in your fear. While this does not take the fear away, it does remove the added pressure of feeling like you are the only one who experiences it.

2. Second, remember that your worth and value are not determined by position or stature. No one remains at

the top forever. Star athletes will eventually lose. Star academics will eventually fade away. Star leaders will eventually become less relevant.

3. Third, focus on staying sharp and serving others well. If your primary motive is stature and success, you will always be looking over your shoulder. If your primary motive is adding value and serving others to the best of your ability, you will reduce fear and increase your influence in the lives of others.

5 Actions That Can Make You "Exceptional"

Everyone wants to be "exceptional." The 15-year-old high school basketball player who aspires to be an NBA player as good as Kevin Durant. The 24-year-old who dreams about becoming a successful entrepreneur like Marcus Lemonis of the TV show *The Profit*. Or perhaps the young woman who aspires to be like Ann Dunwoody, the first woman to become a four-star general in the U.S. Armed Forces. But becoming exceptional doesn't just happen. Here are five things that can help make you exceptional.

1. Invest in your character

You can be one of the best athletes or top business leaders in the country, but if you consistently come up short in your character, you will eventually fail. Pride, arrogance, entitlement, greed, and dishonesty are some of the common character flaws that bring talented people down. Humility, honesty, generosity, and authenticity are some of the character traits that lead to true exceptionality. Remember, every day we are given newsworthy illustrations of very exceptional people doing very dumb things. Avoid this by investing in your character development as much as your talent development.

2. Surround yourself with the right people

Bill Gates said, "Everyone needs a coach. It doesn't matter whether you're a basketball player, a tennis player, a gymnast, or a bridge player." Exceptional people find the best coaches, select great mentors, and stay away from those who will not add positive value to their lives and abilities. Why? Proverbs 22:24-25 tells us that surrounding yourself with the wrong people is like getting caught in a trap! When you surround yourself with the people who add to your life instead of taking away from it, you will be on the path to becoming exceptional.

3. Work extraordinarily hard

There are no shortcuts. Even the most talented people work hard, very hard, at becoming exceptional. Practicing. Taking classes. Reading. Networking. Experimenting. And more practicing. Think of a person who you aspire to be, and you will likely find that they invested extraordinary amounts of time and even money to be their best. There really are no shortcuts to hard work. Average people live vicariously through others (ie. Fantasy Football players – you know who you are!). Exceptional people get off of the couch and work hard!

4. Build on your strengths

Everyone has strengths – they only have to be discovered. Relational. Athletic. Insightful. Mathematical. Verbal. Mechanical. Artistic. These are just a few of the possibilities. Some people have been given extraordinary talent in one or more of these areas. The kind of talent that cannot be developed by only hard work and practice. Regardless of whether you have strengths or super-strengths, build on the strengths you have rather than fixating on what you are not so good at.

5. Develop disciplined focus

I recently watched a documentary about one of the world's top rock climbers. When he was young, his parents were told that he would have difficulty in life because he was developmentally delayed. Over time, he became hyper-focused on conquering some of the most challenging rock walls in the world. His focus was intense! Even after he lost a finger in a saw accident and he was told his climbing days were over, he went on to accomplish climbs that had never been done before. Disciplined focus is the ability to invest serious time and energy to become extraordinary. We call this becoming a laser not a flashlight and it is what differentiates the exceptional from the good.

Sexual Misbehavior Isn't the Only Way to Ruin Your Life & Career

Politicians. Hollywood figures. National news personalities. Professional athletes. College athletes. Coaches. Pastors. Military leaders. Recently, it feels like a big rock is being rolled away and underneath it is a lot of ugly and dirty stuff. The dirt is not new, just newly exposed. We could easily begin to think that sex is now the main culprit in ruining people's lives, but in reality, it is only one way. In fact, the far majority of leaders who ruin themselves do so without inappropriate sexual indulgence. If you want to ruin your life and career, all it takes is doing one or more of these six things.

1. Believe others when they tell you how really, really special you are.

What does a narcissist see when they look in the mirror? Someone who is extraordinary and entitled! Narcissists are people who have an extraordinarily high view of themselves, with an exaggerated view of their uniqueness and strengths which results in extraordinary self-centeredness. They begin to think they are invincible, and before long, they start to act invincible, using and abusing both people and power.

2. Isolate yourself since you are really special.

An isolated leader is a dangerous leader. Why? Because when you are isolated, you lose perspective since you have few people available to help you see yourself more accurately, warn you of danger, and protect you from what you cannot see. Leaders are notorious for isolation. Common self-talk such as "it's lonely at the top" perpetuates and legitimizes isolation, and too much time alone can wreak havoc in the life of a leader.

3. Hone your skill at being a jerk.

We can all be annoying at times, right? Just ask our spouses, children, or co-workers. But there is a difference between being annoying and being a jerk. How do people handle working with a jerk? They avoid them by limiting interaction, escape them by looking for another job, or confront them by telling them, "You're a jerk!" People do not like being around someone who is not nice, and eventually you will face the consequences for how you act.

4. Treat alcohol or drugs like toys rather than guns.

A large number of people consume alcohol or take prescription drugs without abusing them. Yet, many leaders who have behaved badly and made decisions that ruined their lives did so while under the influence. Misused, alcohol and drugs mess with the brain (the source of decision-making) which often results in altering our judgment leading to really bad outcomes.

5. Repeat this phrase often: "It can't happen to me."

If you tell yourself this often enough, you will believe it. I have talked to leaders who thought they would never be the one to have an affair, embezzle, abuse their power, or lose their position, and yet they were. All of us are vulnerable to catastrophic failures and it is only the fool who thinks "I'm better than they are," "I'm smarter than they are," or "I'm more righteous than they are."

6. Ignore input from others. After all, what do they know?

Want to ruin your life real fast? Ignore the counsel of others. Or, just seek input from those who already agree with you. That will make you feel better and allow you to say that you do get input. While too much input can be conflicting and confusing, too little is a sure-fire way to miss out on the insights, warnings, or expertise that can prevent damaging your career.

Every one of us falls short in some area of our lives. But there is a difference between knowing and managing our limitations and shortcomings versus claiming to not have any. I have never met a leader who wanted to intentionally ruin his or her life. But it can happen unless we make every effort to guard against destructive behaviors and to live and lead with a spirit of both teachability and humility.

Questions Every Leader or Owner Should Ask During a Crisis

In a crisis, it is essential to listen and learn. But it is equally important to make sure you are asking yourself, your board, and your team the right questions. Here are 19 questions we believe you should consider when you find yourself in a position of leadership during a crisis. Do not address them all at once; you are already on overload. Instead, reflect on and discuss one or two of these questions every few days.

Personal Questions

1. Am I seeking wise guidance from a limited number of voices including legal, financial, and organizational? (Too many voices will result in static and confusion.)

2. How do my core organizational values shape the decisions I am now considering?

3. How do I guard myself against the natural temptations of acting purely out of fear and self-preservation?

4. How am I showing support for those outside of my organization including sharing best practice ideas, resources, and tangible assistance including goods and/or financial?

5. How am I taking care of my own emotional, spiritual, and physical health?

Staffing Questions

1. What am I or should I consider doing to care for the emotional, financial, spiritual, and physical health of my employees?

2. Do I know which positions are most critical for the present and future of my organization?

3. Do I know which staff I cannot afford to lose and do not want to lose?

4. Am I paying attention to governmental and local social service and faith-based programs that are available to help my employees?

Financial Questions

1. Do I have a clear understanding of my cash-flow, reserves, and line of credit that I have available at this time?

2. Am I aware of the government programs that are available to help organizations like mine?

3. How would I reduce expenses by 10%, 20%, or even 30% while not harming the mission-critical services or products we provide?

4. How do we affirm our mission even more clearly to be a positive solution through this crisis?

Organizational Questions

1. Am I focused on how this crisis can result in new opportunities for my organization?

2. How can this crisis result in new efficiencies for my organization?

3. Who are the key people, internally and externally, whose voices I need to hear and consider as we make adaptive changes?

4. Is the "tyranny of the moment" pulling me and others away from our mission and vision?

5. How am I planning for the health and safety of my employees and constituents during this crisis?

6. What is our plan for continuation of effective operations should this disruption last 30 days? 60 days? 90 days?

Are You Emotionally Tone-Deaf? Here Are 10 Ways to Tell

How would you know if you were blind to your own gaps in emotional intelligence? Here are 10 signs that you might be emotionally tone deaf.

1. People avoid honestly sharing their views with you because of how you might respond.
2. People talk more about you to others than they do directly to you.
3. People do not want to work with you or for you.
4. People see you as negative a majority of the time.
5. People often leave their time with you annoyed or depressed.
6. You are often passed over for a promotion or have trouble finding a new job.
7. You do not smile, make eye contact, or go out of your way to make others feel welcome.
8. You seldom pursue relationships or have others into your home.
9. You have difficulty showing emotion and feel uneasy when others do.
10. You see much of the world in black and white and seldom compromise your position.

If many of these signs of an emotionally tone-deaf leader seem to be true of you, it may be time to examine your strengths and identify areas for growth through a leader 360 feedback assessment.

6 Standard Approaches to Leading

Every leader has a Standard Approach to Leading (SAL). This is the way a leader leads most often and most naturally. While there is no perfect or correct SAL, there can be consequences to each of them. Here are six of the most common Standard Approaches to Leadership.

You CARRY people.

Leaders who use this SAL are known for not holding people accountable. The leader instead chooses to take on another person's responsibilities or place those responsibilities upon others. Carrying others is a good thing when a person is experiencing a difficult season of life. After all, that is what the Bible calls bearing someone's burdens. But it is not good leadership when it happens too often or for too long, especially at work. Other team members can begin to feel penalized by being given even more work, and it can divert the attention of the leader away from things he or she should be doing.

You PUSH people.

This is when a leader uses his or her authority to get people to do what they are not doing or do not want to do. Leaders who use this as their standard approach are known for getting things done but are also known for using intimidation as their go-to technique. There are times when using your positional authority is essential. Sometimes a team member may need a nudge to understand the importance of what is needed and that it is not optional. But when this is your SAL, it will ultimately create a culture of fear rather than long-term performance.

You INSPIRE people.

This one is a bit tricky. After all, who can argue with using inspiration as a motivator? Inspiring leaders do great things, and people love them for it! But if this is ALL a leader does, they may unintentionally shortchange their team because some people are not motivated by inspiration or their response is short-lived. Does inspiration alone motivate your kid to get out of bed, go to school, and pick up the dog poop? If you are an inspiring leader, keep it up but realize you may need a different approach depending on the circumstances and the team members.

You INCLUDE people.

There are many benefits to including others in discussions, idea generation, and even decisions. This is often called a democratic approach. But there are times when a decision needs to be made, and it is needed now, not next month. The leader whose SAL is including may be too insecure, fear taking responsibility, or value being liked by others too highly to make the hard calls.

You MOBILIZE people.

A leader with this SAL is gifted at recruiting talented people, building a great team, and sharing a compelling mission. They create an environment that is attractive to talented people and empowers them to accomplish the vision. What could possibly be wrong with the Mobilizer? When it succeeds, sometimes the leader who mobilized the team can end up harming it because his or her leadership abilities are no longer effective at managing the very growth they helped to produce. And, sadly, there are some leaders who "mobilize" so they do not have to do anything themselves!

You MANIPULATE people.

This is a far more common approach to leadership than some leaders would want to admit. Leaders whose SAL is manipulation commonly compliment and reward those whom they want something from and marginalize or undermine those whom they do not like or do not want to succeed. You often see this in politics, but even organizations like churches and nonprofits are not immune. Some people are wise enough to identify a manipulative leader, but some cannot until they are blindsided and bruised from the painful side effects. While manipulation can seem expedient in the short term, it is never healthy and can quickly ruin the character and reputation of leaders.

So which is your SAL? Perhaps it is hard to pick only one. From my experience, you most likely have one or maybe two that others would use to describe you. But remember, most leaders will use many of these, even if infrequently. And all of them (except for manipulation, of course) have value when used in the right circumstances and with the right people. Proverbs 22:29 says, *"Do you see someone skilled in their work? They will serve before kings; they will not serve before officials of low rank."* The best leaders are skilled in how they lead. They have awareness of themselves, acknowledge their weaknesses, focus on their strengths, and recruit people as good as or better than themselves. Take some time in a team meeting to discuss each of these Standard Approaches to Leadership and perhaps you may find another one or two to add to this list.

Top 10 Ways to Derail Momentum and Growth

Every organization that is experiencing success one day can find itself floundering the next. The following are the top 10 ways it can happen. You have heard it said, "You cannot manage what you do not acknowledge." By understanding these 10 derailers, we can more effectively prevent our organizations from going off the tracks.

1. Success that feeds arrogance which results in a sense of invincibility

In his book *How the Mighty Fall,* author Jim Collins said it best: "Every institution is vulnerable, no matter how great. No matter how much you've achieved, no matter how far you've gone, no matter how much power you've garnered, you are vulnerable to decline. There is no law of nature that the most powerful will inevitably remain on top. Anyone can fall and most eventually do."

2. A team that does not have the right balance of leaders and managers

MANAGERS	LEADERS
• Hold a shorter-term view	• Hold a longer-term view
• Centered on a department	• Centered on the whole organization
• Emphasize policies and procedures	• Emphasize innovation and change
• Focus on revenue allocation	• Focus on revenue generation
• Think tactically	• Think systems

3. "A" level staff and board turning into "B" level staff and board

Marshall Goldsmith said it this way: "What got you here won't get you there." The talent that is required at one size of an organization will seldom suffice as the organization grows. And, when an organization grows faster than the capabilities of its leaders, problems are not far behind. The two greatest determining factors of success will be your competence and your ability to see and lead systems.

4. Erosion of team trust and synergy

Creating and maintaining long-term team health is no easy task. You can easily see and feel erosion in a team culture, but what does it look like when a team has trust and synergy?

- Frequent conversation with a higher ratio of positive over negative interactions
- Agreed-upon expectations and priorities
- Members who have a high level of competency
- A consistent environment of psychological safety
- An atmosphere of fun
- An abundance of flexibility and forgiveness

5. Running on the "bigger and better" leadership treadmill

When success has been experienced, some leaders are driven to do whatever it takes to become even bigger, better, and more well-known. The next growth fad. The next "must attend" seminar. The next leadership book that you must read. But remember to answer the "why" question before the "what." Mechanical treadmills can be life-giving for your heart, but leadership treadmills can be deadly for your spirit.

6. Insufficient capacity for stress

Stress has been demonized. Stress is normal, and it can even be beneficial. And when it becomes unhealthy, it is usually a symptom rather than the problem. There are only two ways to deal with stress - reduce the load or increase your capacity. But remember, a team member's stress is often from other sources beyond work, yet work will often be blamed. Talking about stress with a skilled advisor can actually decrease your stress, which is something all of us can benefit from.

7. Avoidance of candor

Pastor and author Jon Ortberg wisely notes the following about situations where candor is avoided: "When it is withheld, teams deteriorate, performances fail, families break apart, and companies go bankrupt. The lack of appropriate, effective confrontation is fatal to communities, and it can be lethal to individual men and women."

8. Lack of grit

Enduring organizations have gritty leaders. It is grit that often differentiates an organization that prevails from one that diminishes. A gritty leader is someone who has...

- **Passion.** Gritty leaders manifest a passion for what they do.

- **Work.** Gritty leaders work harder than those around them.
- **Delayed Gratification.** Gritty leaders sacrifice short-term gratification.
- **Focus.** Gritty leaders zero in on what they want to accomplish.
- **Perseverance.** Gritty leaders don't easily quit.

9. Formalization that increases bureaucracy and decreases nimbleness

As organizations grow, bureaucracy commonly creeps in, resulting in decreased nimbleness and deadening effects. Common signs of bureaucracy include:

- Oversaturation of policies and rules
- Growing number of decisions that get bogged down
- Decreased risk-taking for fear of getting in trouble
- Policies and procedures taking precedence over solving problems
- Staff and members increasingly seeing the organization as inflexible

10. Focusing more on what is being lost rather than what is being gained

As organizations grow, there are gains, but there are also losses. We would be kidding ourselves to think otherwise. The following are some of the most common losses we hear from clients as well as some of the greatest gains.

GAINS	LOSSES
• More people being served	• Less input on some decisions
• Attracting greater talent	• Farther distance from the top leader(s)
• Greater sense of excitement	• Reporting to new people
• New opportunities for the staff	• Knowing less of what is going on

Derailment often happens ever so slowly. Other times, faster than you thought possible. Leadership is responsible to keep the organization from derailing. How well is your organization doing at staying on the tracks?

5 Daily Actions of Leaders That Will Be Positively Remembered

Think about all of the leaders for whom you have worked. I do not just mean casually think about it, *really* think about it. Write them on a sheet of paper. Or name them in your mind. Carson. Warren. Vince. Bob. Gerry. Kevin. Mike. Gary. Don. Meredith. I could add a lot more – I had A LOT of jobs when I was young! When you were thinking through your list of names, I bet some triggered unkind thoughts because of how little they added to your life, but others gave you pause because of how great they were – how they added energy, value, and positivity to your life. What is fascinating is how many positions I could remember but could not recall for whom I had worked. That says a lot about those leaders.

If you want to be favorably remembered by those you now lead, consider doing these five things – every day.

1. Thank someone every day.

Really simple – find someone who is doing a good job or did something special. Even if it is something small. Small things matter too. Find them and thank them. It is amazing how often we forget to do this and how great it feels to others when we acknowledge them.

2. Help someone every day.

When we moved into new offices, the only thing that made it successful was all of the help that we received from a number of people. Helping is powerful because it is so tangible. So, who can you help today? Provide help on a project. Solve a problem. Give additional resources. Whatever the "it" is, be helpful. It will be remembered.

3. Encourage someone every day.

Do you realize how bad people feel most days? It may not be visible, but, on the inside, they are carrying the stresses of life and work. Family and finances. Health and hurt. An encouraging word or action can provide fuel for another hour or another day. A cupcake on the desk. A note of appreciation. It will be remembered.

4. Pray for someone every day.

Over 70% of people in the United States pray at least weekly. So, if you are reading this, the odds are that you periodically pray. While it may be a stretch to pray for someone daily, give it a try. Most people, even those with little religious connection, appreciate someone praying for them, especially when life gets tough and the pressures are squeezing in from all sides.

5. Be grateful for something every day.

This one is different than the others. It focuses on the way we think, not just what we do. This matters so much because when we consider what we are grateful for every day, it changes our attitude, increases our joy, and reduces our negativity. And that will be remembered.

How to Know You Are NOT a Narcissistic Leader

What is a narcissist? The simple answer: you know when you meet one or work for one! Psychologists Alan Cavaiola and Neil Lavender said that after being around a narcissist, you will often feel demeaned, inadequate, unappreciated, and angry. Narcissism is when a person has an extraordinarily high view of oneself and falls far short on empathy towards others. Psychologists have tested a number of college students over the past 30 years and have noted a continuous increase in narcissism during this time. So, rather than asking ourselves if we are one – let's look at how to know that you are NOT one.

1. If you are known more for building others up than tearing others down – you are less likely to be a narcissist.

2. If you understand and acknowledge your flaws and limitations rather than exaggerate your strengths and value to the organization – you are less likely to be a narcissist.

3. If you give credit to others rather than take it all yourself – you are less likely to be a narcissist.

4. If you name drop to add value to a conversation rather than to look good – you are less likely to be a narcissist.

5. If you invest in others rather than take advantage of them for your own benefit – you are less likely to be a narcissist.

6. If you both feel empathy and show empathy towards others – you are less likely to be a narcissist.

7. If you look out for the interest of others rather than acting as though you are entitled to more than others – you are less likely to be a narcissist.

Seldom do any of us leaders know how we are doing in these seven areas without feedback from truthful colleagues, friends, and coaches. We would all do well to remember the wise words from Ann Landers: "Don't accept your dog's admiration as conclusive evidence that you are wonderful."

6 Signs of Your Organization's Shadow Side & How to Contain It

Every organization has a visible side and a somewhat invisible side, also known as the shadow side. This is the unhealthy, underlying organization within the organization. Sometimes the shadow side is inactive, like a dormant cancer cell in the body. When it is inactive, it is somewhat harmless. But when it becomes active, things can get ugly very fast. Here are the warning signs of an active shadow side and what to do to advance the health of the organization.

1. **Growing organizational secrecy** – more people talking in hallways, in parking lots, and on social media than in actual meetings.

2. **Increasing staff turnover** – more people quietly searching and ultimately leaving by their own choice.

3. **Increasing "chatter"** – more people talking, venting, and sometimes gossiping to one another about the culture and leadership.

4. **Difficulty in recruitment** – fewer talented people accepting offers for key positions.

5. **Avoidance of difficult discussions** – fewer candid conversations in team and board meetings.

6. **Surprising decisions, actions, or words** – more people thinking "what was that all about" or "where did that come from?"

What to do about the shadow side?

Most organizations and leaders have experienced the shadow side becoming active or will experience it soon enough. As challenging as it can be, it is not uncommon. Rather than reacting, learn. The shadow side will not go away by yelling, threatening, or inflaming suspicion. A wise leader will contain their fear and seek to learn. Here are six suggestions to start the process of bringing your organization back to health.

1. First, acknowledge that the shadow side exists.

2. Ask questions in a non-threatening way.

3. Seek help by asking a neutral adviser to look at the culture and make recommendations.

4. Contain the temptation to punish those you feel are "against you" unless it's confirmed they are toxic.

5. Seek first to understand rather than to prove yourself or defend yourself.

6. Be humble enough to acknowledge where you and the organizational culture can improve.

The Influential Leader

Few things are more energizing than getting to watch a gifted leader at work. And, few things are more irritating than watching an incompetent person pretend to lead! Here at The Center Consulting Group, our team of leadership consultants and coaches regularly have the honor of working with exemplary leaders. These are men and women who have influence – which is the capacity to have a significantly positive effect on people or situations. Influential leaders have a healthy blend of ability complemented by confidence. The following graphic is a simple matrix to identify four types of leaders. Where are you? And where are the members of your team?

- **Delusional Leader:** This leader possesses an unwarranted confidence in his abilities but without any evidence to back it. *Action needed:* Respectfully and candidly confront his lack of awareness.
- **Inadequate Leader:** This is a sad picture of a leader. Lacking both abilities as well as confidence, she does not lead at all. *Action needed:* Invest in her development or reposition her.
- **Untapped Leader:** The untapped leader has abilities far greater than he can see but lacks the confidence needed to influence. *Action needed:* Affirm his abilities and coach him in building confidence.
- **Influential Leader:** This leader has proven abilities and a humble confidence that has emerged as a result of her impact. *Action needed:* Maximize her influence to fuel the vision.

For the sake of clarity, I will state the obvious – none of us are influential leaders all of the time. We all lack some self-awareness and have untapped potential. However, when we consistently enhance our abilities and manifest humble confidence, our positive influence on both people and organizations will grow. While we may have some raw, natural talent, we need to work at it and work with it. And false humility seldom produces good outcomes. All of our abilities are directly or indirectly a gift from God, and therefore we can be confident in using those talents for positive purposes.

5 Positive Ways Suffering Shapes Us

The Bible says it and life proves it – everyone will experience some hurt. It is only a matter of when, not if. Most of us have an internal GPS that is programmed to avoid suffering whenever we can, but that is not possible. Life happens! You receive a diagnosis of cancer. A spouse cheats on you. A child is born with autism. A car accident takes the life of a loved one. A chronic medical illness drains what little savings you have. Suffering is part of life. Yet, with suffering comes both struggle and opportunity. There is no doubt that we will be shaped by the suffering we experience. That experience can, and often does, make us better… much better. Here are five positive ways suffering can shape you.

1. Empathy

Suffering will help you have a greater understanding of those around you who are experiencing the hardships of life. When you look at people, you will often see things that others do not. When a team member has a personal hardship like difficulty in their marriage, a struggling child, or a major health crisis, you will not only SEE it… you will FEEL it. That feeling creates the connection of empathy.

2. Emotional Muscle

You do not build physical muscle without some pain and stress, just like you do not build emotional muscle without some suffering and hardship. While suffering can sometimes cause us to overload and break, it can also make us stronger… much stronger. When we realize that we were able to endure it, we are stronger for the next time suffering emerges in our lives, and we also serve as a source of hope for others who are feeling, "I will never survive this."

3. Team

Suffering, more than anything else, will teach us the importance of having a team around us. In the Bible, one writer put it this way: "Pity the person who has no one to help them," Ecclesiastes 4. Taking an extra shift. Giving a ride. Providing a meal. Cutting the lawn. Giving a gift card. Or simply saying, "How are you doing and how can I help?" The power of team is never understood at its greatest level until we experience suffering.

4. Focus

When a major life challenge hits, we can learn about the importance of prioritizing. In other words, what is most important in my life, family, and job and what is least important. Spending time on frivolous activities and timewasters is no longer an option. Survival requires focus on those things that are most important while allowing things that are least important to either be deleted, delegated, or at least postponed.

5. Transparency

In the *Harvard Business Review* article "Why Should Anyone Be Led By You?," Robert Goffee and Gareth Jones stress the importance for leaders to be more vulnerable. They note that by doing so, those around us will see that we are "genuine and approachable—human and humane." Too often, leaders live in costume, like every day is Halloween. Suffering provides us with the opportunity to be transparent. When wisely managed, such vulnerability will increase trust, camaraderie, and opportunities for those around us to realize we are just mere mortals too.

7 Leadership Labels: Which Are True of You?

Leaders are complicated people. To think a single word can describe us would be the definition of over-simplification. But we all do have patterns and tendencies that result in a word or two (or three) becoming the labels for which we are known. Here are seven of the most common leadership labels we have seen. Some are not so nice. Others are much more appealing. Which ones best reflect you?

1. Inspiration

"There is something exciting ahead, and we can attain it!" Inspirational leaders are known for using the power of vision, words, and stories to motivate others to accomplish something great. Their charisma is motivating, and their picture of the future is energizing – resulting in a lot of energy and passion.

2. Intimidation

"I am more powerful than you." Leaders who lead by way of intimidation are known for using anger, threat, and general meanness to get you to do what they want. This may not sound appealing, but it is more prevalent than you may think.

3. Relationship

"I value you and enjoy connecting with you." These are leaders who use care, truth, and connection to form relational capital. This capital allows people to follow them and want to support them by choice rather than by force.

4. Knowledge

"I am the expert here." Knowledge-based leaders have expertise, and that expertise provides them with the ability to guide others. In other words, they know something others do not, and everyone is not an equal when it comes to knowledge.

5. Position

"I am the boss." If you have ever heard a leader say, "You report to me so do what I tell you!", this is a leader who is using his or her position as the primary motivator to get a team member to act. Positional leaders have a legitimate claim since they do have the position, but it seldom will result in long-term health and performance.

6. Policy

"Policies are vital and must be followed above all else." These leaders are policy centric. They feel strongly that policies are there for a reason and everyone must follow them. Period. No exceptions. Such leaders have a point. There certainly are some policies that should never be compromised... never! However, not all policies are equal in importance. And if all we needed was policies, there would be no need for leaders or discernment - all we would need is a policy manual and policy enforcers.

7. Service

"My primary goal is to help you to be successful." Leaders who lead by way of service are not as concerned about position, title, or policy. They just want to help those who report to them be their best and help the organization or team they lead to be its best. What they may lack in charisma, they make up for in service.

6 Times When You Should NOT Make a Decision

Making good decisions not only requires wise counsel and accurate information, it also requires knowing when to make a decision and when to hold off. Here are six times when it is better to delay a decision until you are in a better state to make it.

1. When you are really angry.

Anger is a powerful emotion, and it can skew our thinking in such a way that we say or do things we would not normally do. Proverbs 14:17 says a quick-tempered person does foolish things, and it's likely we all have firsthand experience with this! So, when you are really angry, it is wise to wait before you act or speak.

2. When you are exhausted.

Fatigue can result in making decisions that may feel right at that moment of exhaustion but may not feel so good once the fatigue has lifted. So, when you are feeling burned-out, be careful regarding the decisions you choose to make.

3. When you are unusually anxious.

Anxiety can be brutal. It can take your mind captive and overwhelm your judgment. Such anxiety can be so distressing that people will make any decision just to end it. However good it may feel at the moment, such decisions are often regretted later on when the anxiety is ratcheted down. So, take extra caution when making decisions while battling a bout of anxiety.

4. When you just experienced a major loss.

A major loss such as the death of someone special, a divorce, or a diagnosis of a life-threatening illness often reshapes our normal thought processes. Such powerful life events can lead us to make impulsive decisions - ones that we will regret later on after a "new normal" returns. Financial planners, lawyers, and psychologists often remind their clients to not make any major decisions immediately after a traumatic life event.

5. When someone you highly trust is opposed.

When you have great trust in someone, it does not imply you will *never* go against their advice, but it does mean you should take a pause and give further thought regarding why they are opposing or cautioning you. We are counseled to "turn our ear towards wisdom," Proverbs 5:1. While this does not mean that the person who is opposed is right, it does mean that you better make sure you know you are.

6. When you feel extraordinarily great.

Nothing feels more energizing than a big win or a great success. It is at such times that you likely feel a sense of exuberance, excitement, and confidence. These are some of the fun aspects of success. But success can also breed over-confidence, and even arrogance, that can result in decisions built on a faulty foundation. While the emotions that follow success are to be enjoyed, don't let them deceive you.

5 Types of People You Will Encounter in Life

We encounter many types of people in life, including at work as well as in our social networks. Some we cannot live without, and others we would like to live without. Here are the most common types of people and what to do with each. Many people are a hybrid of two or more.

Drainers: those who deplete your emotional tank

How do you spot a drainer? You are exhausted just thinking about your upcoming meeting with them. Drainers are not necessarily bad people; they are just very needy and can drain your emotional tank faster than you can refill it.

What to do with Drainers? You cannot and should not avoid Drainers – just limit your time with them.

Sustainers: those who replenish your emotional tank

Sustainers are truly a gift from God. After even a short time with them, you feel encouraged and confident. Whether it is by their humor, encouragement, or enjoying a hobby together, Sustainers add value to your life and overall health. We all need at least one or two Sustainers in our lives, or the Drainers will drain us dry!

What to do with Sustainers? Don't become a Drainer to them!

Trainers: those who add wisdom and counsel to your life

Mentor. Coach. Friend. Teacher. There should be people in our lives we can count on for wise advice. Proverbs 1:5 says it well – wise people seek counsel. A Sustainer and Trainer can be found in the same person, but not always. Trainers don't need to be encouraging as much as they need to be wise and knowledgeable.

What to do with a Trainer? Listen to them or they will stop being a Trainer in your life!

Criticizers: those who consistently find what is wrong with you

Criticizers are heat-seeking missiles and you are the target! The difference between a person who provides you with truthful feedback and a criticizer is often the volume. In most conversations, Criticizers lead with finding what is wrong with you, your leadership, the weather, room temperature, a sore foot, etc. You get the point. And yes, criticizers often carry the Drainer virus!

What to do with a Criticizer? Limit exposure if possible. If it's not possible (because they are a spouse, boss, etc.), try to talk to them about it.

Users: those who just use others for their own purposes

Users are utilitarian in that you are a means to their ends. They are not "in a relationship" with you, but rather want something from you. Money. Promotion. Access. Tasks. Their interaction with you is based upon what they need from you, otherwise, you seldom hear from them. They are often shrewd and manipulative, having honed this craft from their early days and family experiences.

What to do with a User? Be on guard and do not expect anything from them regarding a relationship.

While we would all like to see ourselves as Sustainers and Trainers, it is likely that in some contexts, we are seen differently. It is not easy or fun to have someone think of us as Drainers, Criticizers, or Users. But we can aspire to lead well by looking at ourselves with a more accurate perspective, seeking feedback from others, and disciplining ourselves to live in such a way that we have a positive influence on those around us.

When to Quit & When You Should Think Twice

The toughness of Navy Seals has become well known through movies like Lone Survivor and American Sniper. Becoming part of this elite group requires surviving grueling tests of mental, emotional, and physical toughness. And then there is the infamous bell. The bell is ever present while the Seal trainees endure the intense exercises; and all they must do to quit and receive a nice meal, hot shower, and clean bed is to ring it three times. I have read a few excellent books and seen some great movies on the Navy Seals, and while I was inspired by their endurance, at the age of 60, I was ready to ring the bell while just reading about the stress, let alone actually experiencing it!

So, when is it the right time to quit and ring the bell in your life, and when it is better to think twice?

Don't quit...

1. Just because it's difficult.

Difficulty and stress are a normal part of life. It is unrealistic to expect a stress-free or disappointment-free life! In addition, extremely challenging times often only last for a season and seldom become permanent.

2. When you are angry.

Anger resides in the laps of fools. Those are wise words from the book of Ecclesiastes in the Bible. Have you ever seen anger result in good decisions? Me neither. So, don't quit when you are ticked off, or you will likely regret it.

3. Because you didn't get what you want.

If we quit every time we do not get what we want, we will be quitting a lot! Not getting the promotion or raise or not being recognized the way we feel we should can be disappointing but may not justify quitting.

4. When you are fatigued.

Fatigue can be brutal. We have all experienced those nasty emotions after not getting enough sleep or dealing with a lot of stress. During Seal training, candidates would encourage one another so they would not ring the bell due to fatigue.

5. To get even or make a point.

Sometimes we either quit or threaten to do so in order to make a point or to punish someone, like a boss or even a spouse. While it may feel cathartic at the moment, it usually results in regrets and embarrassment.

Consider quitting...

1. When it is too toxic.

There is such a thing as "too toxic." Serious risks to your physical or mental wellbeing are legitimate reasons to ring the bell. Even cancer patients sometimes have to forego a chemo treatment because their bodies cannot handle it.

2. When you have a much better opportunity.

If we never quit anything, most of us would not be where we are today. If I did not leave teaching at a college (a position I really enjoyed), I would not have started The Center Consulting Group (a greater opportunity for innovation and impact). Passion, fresh opportunity, and better use of our gifts are all worthy considerations for quitting.

3. When your circumstances justify it.

You need to earn more money to provide for your family. Your aging parents need more help. The needs of a spouse or child require that you have a different work arrangement. Sometimes circumstances do justify a change.

4. When staying will require violating your integrity.

In the book *Bad Blood,* the company Theranos recruited a lot of very smart people but many of them were asked to shade the truth or just plain lie. When some pushed back, they were fired. Others quit rather than compromise their integrity.

5. When wise counsel affirms it.

Here at The Center Consulting Group, we say it so often we should have it tattooed on our arms – wise people seek counsel (Proverbs 15:22). If you are thinking of quitting something important like a relationship, job, or even a church, seek counsel first!

5 Reasons Why Toxic Leaders Get Away With It

How do nasty leaders and managers get away with being toxic? And sometimes, the worse they behave, the more money they earn! According to a longitudinal study[8] done in the U.S., researchers found that leaders (both men and women) across many occupations and positions who were disagreeable earned more than those who were agreeable.[9] While I cannot explain all of the "whys" behind this, from the years The Center Consulting Group has provided coaching to businesses, churches, and nonprofits, I have a few ideas. Here are five reasons why toxic leaders get away with their behavior and can even make more money.

1. The Power of Celebrity Status

How do celebrities sometimes get away with treating others so poorly? People will allow the poor behaviors because they want to be accepted by and benefit from those with status. Even infamous celebrities like Bonnie and Clyde, who were known for multiple robberies and for murdering nine police officers and several other people, had a large crowd of people rush their bullet-ridden car to see the bodies and grab a sick souvenir. No one ever said the power of celebrity makes sense!

---

8 Timothy Judge, Beth Livingston, Charlice Hurst. "Do Nice Guys-and Gals-Really Finish Last? The Joint Effects of Sex and Agreeableness on Income," *Journal of Personality and Social Psychology*. 2011.

9 Rachel Emma Silverman, "Hey, You! Mean People Earn More, Study Finds," *The Wall Street Journal*. Aug. 15, 2011. www.wsj.com/articles/SB10001424053111904823804576502763895892974.

2. Fear of Financial Armageddon

Top performers, including in business, sports, politics, and church, are often given greater permissions because of the fear of the possible financial losses that could occur without them. Sometimes this fear is real, and these people are often referred to as "the rainmakers." Other times it is exaggerated. But either way, we have seen this fear result in far more permissions for bad behavior than others in the organization could get away with. And, even worse, rewarded with greater compensation!

3. A Board That Is Oblivious

Nonprofit organizations, such as churches and hospitals, and publicly held companies are required to have a governing board. One of the primary jobs of a board is to make sure the organization is healthy, and the leader is leading well. This is no easy task since boards are not involved day to day and often lack accurate information. However, if a leader gets caught in toxic behavior, an oblivious board will become both sobered and embarrassed very quickly.

4. Supervisors Who Are Just Like Them

Kids often use the phrase "it takes one to know one" when trading verbal blows with others. If a supervisor is known for being a bit toxic, it is hard for them to see the toxic person they supervise as a problem – after all, they are looking at themselves! A supervisor who often assumes the worst, leads with "no," or is constantly critical may not see it as a problem when one of their team is doing the same.

5. The Owner's Wall of Protection

Owners are those who either started a business, bought one, or inherited the position from their family. Without an outside group of advisers or a professional coach, such owners can be walled off from feedback that would give them greater awareness of how they are perceived. In contrast to a publicly held company or even a nonprofit, a privately held business doesn't even need to prove its profitability so long as the owner(s) is satisfied.

The Antidotes for Toxic Behavior

The number one antidote for toxic behavior is FEEDBACK. Feedback is the only way we can have an accurate view of ourselves. With the guidance of a professional coach, honest and anonymous feedback can be a powerful force for change.

A second antidote is having guiding values that espouse character, people, and effectiveness. A focus on only one of these will usually result in an organization or team that is out of balance, eventually wobbling or even crashing.

"Trust Who?" What to Do When You Lose Trust in Others

I recently opened a loaf of bread, and the first slice in the bag had a slight problem... MOLD! In the past, I would have tossed the entire loaf in the trash, treating the whole bag as contaminated even though it was usually only one or two pieces that were affected and the rest were fine. Perhaps this rings true of how our trust in authority works. In much of society today, if trust were a football game, it would be a thrashing, with trust on the losing team. On any given day, you can read about or listen to the symptoms of the erosion of trust, especially as it relates to anything institutional in nature. A lot of this erosion has been caused by high profile examples of authority being abused and people being victimized.

But one of the downsides of the constant presence of social media, in general, and news, in particular, is how a small number of cases where power or position were abused were then given an extraordinary amount of attention. And, like the moldy slice of bread, this hyper-attention can lead us to believe that every leader in that profession or institution is bad when that is seldom the case. Most doctors really do care about their patients. Most pastors are seeking to genuinely help their congregation. There are politicians who genuinely care about how to help their constituents. There are police officers that both care about and sacrifice for their communities. And many managers are looking out for the good of their employees. There are certainly consequences to placing our trust in leaders that squander it, but there are also devastating consequences in refusing to trust at all. So, what are we supposed to do when we lose trust in others?

1. Choose trust over cynicism.

When someone violates our trust, it leaves a nasty bruise. The alternative is to never trust again, but that does not sound like a very good option. Do you really want to live in a community or work in a company where you are suspicious of every decision that is made and question every motive that is in play? We have to make a choice to either start fresh with trust or allow cynicism and suspicion to rule our lives and relationships. When you see your trust declining in regards to another person or organization, above all, resist all-or-nothing thinking. Do not withhold all of your trust from any individual or group *or* grant all of your trust to them. Resist allowing cynicism and suspicion to rule you.

2. Watch your daily intake of information.

Hanging around a lot of cynical people? Listening to a particular commentator all of the time? Following bloggers who are one-dimensional in their message and thoughts? Some people make a living out of providing a constant diet of critique, and it does not matter if they have any expertise since that is no longer a qualifying trait to share your opinions. I recently learned of a book about church leadership written by someone who has never led a successful church. But the lack of credentials does not matter as long as there are people who chose to listen. Like an exemplary athlete who carefully watches his or her diet, smart leaders carefully choose the source of their information and the amount they ingest.

3. Test assumptions – especially your own.

Every one of us has assumptions or things we believe are true, underlying how we think about things. And our ultimate assumption is that we see things accurately. Multiple people can see the same car accident and have very different recollections of what happened. It would be hard to convince them that what they saw was incomplete or inaccurate. When you find yourself starting to distrust someone, test your assumptions. Ask yourself, "How do I know my thoughts or perceptions are correct?" and, "Why do others see this person or situation differently than I do?" It is easy to test the assumptions of others, but it is much wiser to first test our own.

4. Pursue relationships.

Yes, there are people I don't like. I doubt that comes as a surprise to you since I am confident there are people that you don't like too. The way they lead others, talk to others, or act around others feeds the distrust you have towards them. And the less we trust someone, the more we try to distance ourselves from them which results in even deeper distrust. Years ago, I met a leader that I did not like. (I had my reasons, even if they weren't all that good). A few years later, I had the opportunity to spend more time with this person and learn more about them. We ended up becoming great friends and confidants. So, when you find someone that you do not trust, such as a team member, neighbor, or boss, resist the natural tendency to move away from them and instead proactively pursue a relationship with them.

5. Hold yourself to the same standard you hold others to.

Most of us expect others to show us grace when we make a mistake. When we disappoint others, we want them to resist the urge to add it to the permanent record they hold in their minds. But if we are honest with ourselves, we are sometimes less than willing to do the same towards others. I recently read this interesting story about Abraham Lincoln. During the Civil War, Lincoln and his assistant John Hay were waiting for General McClellan to arrive at his home to talk with him. When McClellan did arrive, he walked past them and went upstairs to bed, completely ignoring the President! And he worked for the President! John Hay was insulted and asked Lincoln what he was going to do about it. The President let it go saying it was "better at this time not to be making points of etiquette and personal dignity." In other words, don't make every insult or slight a 10. We want others to show us grace, and we would be smart to offer the same unto others.

We live in a very imperfect world made up of imperfect people. So, it comes as no surprise that our trust in others, including leaders and authority figures, may be damaged. But that does not mean it needs to remain that way nor that it cannot be improved. If you want to grow trust, give these five practices a try. And whatever you do, don't throw out all of the bread just because of a little mold!

How to Become a Visionary Leader

While visiting a long-time client and touring the ministry he has been leading for almost 30 years, I thought, "Here is an exemplary visionary leader in action." I would estimate that well over half a million young people have been influenced by this organization's vision to inspire youth to shape their world. Here are eight things this visionary leader does that you can implement into your leadership.

1. Dream.

Above all, visionary leaders are dreamers. They love to think about what is not yet and what can be. This reflects what I have seen in this leader for many years – dreaming about how to reach more young people, how to raise up more leaders, and how to have the greatest impact for Christ and his mission.

2. Share inspiring stories.

Have you ever listened to someone, and the next thing you know, an hour has gone by and you didn't even realize it? You begin to feel you are part of the story and the vision starts to inspire you! That is what this leader does – telling true and inspiring stories that capture your heart as much as your head.

3. See things others do not see.

While driving around the 1,000-acre lakefront property with state-of-the-art facilities, this leader shared stories of how it came to be and pointed out areas that are not yet what they should be. He would look at something and say

"See that? That has got to change!" He was not a mystic, but he did have the gift to see what so many others could not.

4. Invest in and empower others.

Visionary leaders not only see what can be regarding properties and programs, they also see the same potential in people. They invest in those people and allow them to lead. This leader said, "We take 19-year-olds and entrust both peers and over 300 kids to each of them – and they learn to have real responsibility… and lead!" Over the years, many of these young people have gone on to positions of serious influence and leadership.

5. Honor others.

Visionary leaders often get all of the credit for success. But good visionary leaders are humble enough to know that it never could happen without their team. Everywhere we went, this leader introduced us to different staff members by name and honored them, sharing what they do and how well they do it. From the chef to the maintenance staff, he honored them all.

6. Make tough decisions.

Having a vision is one thing. Making it happen is entirely different. This visionary leader has made many tough decisions over the years regarding programs, staffing, and finances. Such decisions can produce conflict and result in disappointment. But visionary leaders are willing to make hard decisions if they believe it is in the best interest of the mission.

7. Take risks.

If there is no risk present, there is no vision. Visionary leaders are willing to take risks. Some leaders are reckless in the name of vision. But good visionary leaders, like this one, seek counsel and listen to others. And when it comes down to it, they are willing to make a decision, often without any guarantees for success, because they know it is an even greater risk to do nothing.

8. Manifest humble authenticity.

In the first 30 minutes of watching this visionary leader share with his staff, he talked about his own weaknesses and vulnerabilities. That immediately set a culture where it's ok to not be perfect and one where authenticity is affirmed. Sometimes, visionary leaders try to present an image of strength and infallibility. But this leader didn't. He humbly and courageously shared his brokenness in front of a whole group of new staff as well as us, his guests.

Who We Are

We are 100% focused on leaders.
With Christian values as our organization's foundation, our mission is to help leaders in businesses, nonprofits, and churches lead well.

We make you our first priority.
We have nothing to gain by "selling" you services you do not need.

We customize our services for you.
Our team of experienced consultants and staff customizes services for you and your organization's needs.

We listen and learn to help you lead.
We make sure we fully understand your unique context, vision, and needs before we recommend the services we believe will provide the solutions for your needs.

We build long-lasting relational connections.
We stay connected to many of our clients long after the contract has ended. In fact, many of our clients have contracted with us multiple times over many years.

We not only provide solutions, we help you implement them.
Our consultants work with you and your other leaders by providing ongoing coaching, encouragement, and accountability to increase your success.

Our Solutions

- Executive Coaching
- Leader and Staffing Assessment
- Leadership Development
- Communications and Marketing Advising
- Succession Planning
- Crisis Guidance
- Action Planning
- Staffing Guidance
- H.R. Guidance
- Personalized Coaching Retreats
- Board/Owner Advising
- Organizational Structure
- New Market Assessment and Development
- Merger/Acquisition Guidance and Coaching

Fees

The Center Consulting Group is a nonprofit organization. Our fees are determined by the services you request and your ability to pay. Don't let fees prevent you from contacting us. We will do all we can to find a workable solution for you.

Contact Us

To learn more about how our team can assist you, please contact us at **215-723-2325** or visit our website, **www.centerconsulting.org.**

Assessment Tools

Leader 360° Process
This process includes gathering anonymous perspectives of how your leadership is viewed by you, your supervisor(s), your peers, and those who report to you. Such feedback is one of the most accurate ways to identify strengths, areas of improvement, and possible blind spots.

Personality Testing
Our personality assessments provide a variety of insights into an individual's behaviors, motivators, strengths, areas of development, traditional personality traits, and job-centered behavioral characteristics. They can be used for both pre-hire screening and coaching an employee or team of employees.

Employee Performance Review
Our easy and accurate web-based process collects and computes feedback between the employee and his or her manager to encourage meaningful feedback. This process promotes a fair and open discussion about how to maximize the strengths of each team member.

Group Assessments
Board Assessment: Includes a survey and/or confidential phone interviews of board members to identify strengths, perceptions, and areas of improvement.
Employee Satisfaction Survey: Includes a survey of your employees to identify perceptions regarding job satisfaction, benefits, morale, and other themes.

Organizational Health Assessment
This assessment includes our custom-designed surveys, confidential interviews, and facilitated discussions about your organizational health and the relational health of your team to give you objectivity and foresight in making wise decisions.

Endorsements

“Attentive, responsive, and great question-askers. The Center Consulting Group has provided a critically valuable outside perspective that our organization desperately needed. Bolstered by decades of experience in organizational leadership, The Center's consultants took the time to understand us and our organizational needs. From there, they assisted us in discovering our culture, untangling our growth issues, and developing a healthy strategic plan. They are making us better leaders.” –Center Client

“My time with my coach was engaging, thought-provoking, and action-oriented. I would recommend The Center Consulting Group to anyone looking to take the next step in their field – whatever that step might be.” –Center Client

“The consultants at The Center Consulting Group are thorough, objective, and wise in their approach. Having outside voices from The Center has changed the dynamics of our leadership conversations for the better and has helped us move through many challenges over the years. We are incredibly grateful for their help and support.” –Center Client

“The team at The Center Consulting Group provides steady council that is wise, energizing, timely, and highly customized. Their coaching brings tremendous value by encouraging robust discussion among our leadership team, always maintaining focus on the mission and values of our organization. They have walked alongside us as we navigated several significant structural and strategic changes over the years.” –Center Client

About the Author

Jay Desko is the Executive Director of The Center Consulting Group located in Dublin, Pennsylvania. Jay has also served in senior leadership positions at Calvary Church in Souderton, Pennsylvania for over 25 years. Jay brings experience in the areas of organizational assessment, leadership coaching, decision-making, and strategic questioning. Jay's degrees include an M.Ed. in Instructional Systems Design and a Ph.D. in Organizational Behavior and Leadership. If you would like to contact Jay, he can be reached at jdesko@centerconsulting.org.